Growing Up
ALASKAN

RONDA STILLEY KOTELCHUCK

Dedication and Acknowledgments

This book is dedicated to my warm and wonderful family: Dave Kotelchuck, my ever-supportive husband, my two daughters, Tamar and Shana, their husbands, Nathan Hendrie and Myron Dorfman, our grandchildren, Julia Hendrie, Asa and Yael Dorfman and our step-grandchildren, Erik, Viviana and Efrem Dorfman. It is also dedicated to my sister, Lynn Stilley and her daughter Jeannette Wheatley; to my brother Alan Stilley, his wife Pat and daughters Megan and Dana.

Finally, I want to acknowledge and thank Judith Hannan, my writing mentor; the Invisible Ink Program of Memorial Sloane Kettering Cancer Center, which encouraged me to undertake this project; Amy Rosenberg, my copyeditor; and Elizabeth Sheehan, who helped produce the book.

Table of
CONTENTS

PREFACE

What follows is a mix of autobiography, memoir, and stories of growing up, first in New Mexico, but largely in Alaska, mostly in the 1950s. So different was my childhood from all that followed that I wanted to capture and share it, at least for family and friends. It begins with sketches of the main characters — my mother and father, whose values and effort shaped our family culture and legacy. It is organized in rough chronological blocks, usually corresponding to where we were living at the time. The stories end in 1964, when I graduated from college and left Alaska for the last time, although the account includes an epilogue updating the main characters. The stories are, of course, told through my eyes as a growing child and as I remember them, recognizing that memory is a notoriously tricky affair, especially as we age.

My parents,
Bill Stilley
and Velma
Stroope,
during their
college
years.

PROLOGUE

The Characters

My father, William (Bill) Stilley, was born in 1918 and raised on a farm near Ft. Smith, Arkansas, the second youngest of six children. His mother suffered from mental illness that left him traumatized and estranged from his family, and he was raised largely by two aunts. He left home early in his adolescence, during the Depression, initially spending time with his favorite aunt in Kremmling, Colorado, and then making his way independently, holding various jobs in Colorado and New Mexico. In 1940, at the age of 26, he enrolled in New Mexico State A&M (Agriculture and Mechanical Arts, later renamed New Mexico State) with the intent of becoming a civil engineer. His family subsequently relocated to California and his siblings all attended college and became professionals, while he followed a similar course but without family support.

He initially told my mother he had no family, leaving her "madder than the dickens" as she used to say, when she found out otherwise. Letters from his family, when they caught up with us, would sit unopened for weeks until my mother, fearing news of deaths or family disasters, opened them. He never discussed the most formative experiences of his life — details we would have wanted to know about his childhood, his birth family, the interlude that followed his leaving home and his experiences in the Army during World War II. All I know of these events is what my mother told me and what I learned in letters from his two aunts after his death.

My mother, Velma Stroope, was born in 1923 and raised with her older sister on a sheep ranch in Corona, New Mexico, a small town (the population peaked just after WWII at 3,000), located in the geographic dead center of New Mexico and dubbed the "pinto-bean capital of the world." Velma's childhood is the story of losses. At the age of one she lost her mother, Ollie Sloane Stroop, who died of pneumonia after a three-day blizzard during which Ollie was left alone to tend the children and the livestock while her husband Bert helped search for a neighbor missing in the storm.

Following Ollie's death, my mother was raised by her paternal grandmother, who, by everyone's account, was a cruel and abusive woman. My mother had few memories of this period (and her sister's memories were so bad that she wouldn't share them). Bert then re-married and Velma dearly loved her new stepmother, Florence Clayman. Then, at the age of nine, she lost her father Bert to a horsing accident. Her stepmother subsequently married John Potter whom my mother could not abide. John was by all accounts a lazy, deceitful, abusive man who believed he was marrying into inheritance of the ranch. The marriage forced a wedge between my mother and Florence and thus she effectively lost her stepmother and became an orphan.

At the age of eighteen, she followed her sister, Hivana, to Las Cruces where she enrolled in home economics at New Mexico A&M—and where she met my father. Both lived in the dorms and ate in a family style, co-ed dining hall where, in true Depression-era style, food was in short supply. Her crude and selfish tablemates refused to pass her food, while my father was polite and protective. She was impressed. After dinner, students, still hungry, walked some distance to a local store and my father, one of the few students who owned a car, began giving my mother a ride. Romance blossomed. They married in August 1942, keeping it a secret because my father's job as a dorm counsellor required that he be single.

Both were children of the Depression. Both found themselves alone in the world, but now they had each other. They started with virtually nothing, although their families were never at the bottom rungs of the economic ladder. Both were strivers — smart, independent, aspiring — and our early family life was built entirely around my parents' efforts to secure themselves economically and assure that their children had every opportunity in life.

Less than a year after they married, while my mother was pregnant with me, the Japanese bombed Pearl Harbor and my father enlisted in the infantry — without her consent. My mother was furious and frightened, as the prospect of combat threatened yet another loss — one which would again leave her alone in the world but this time with an infant to raise. I was born while my father was in basic training at Camp Roberts, California, and he saw me once at three months old before shipping off to Europe.

With my birth, my mother now had someone in her life to replace all of those who had been or might yet be lost. This set the stage for a very close and intimate relationship when I was young. I adored her. She was my champion and advocate, sometimes to excess. She was warm, sensitive, interested and emotionally attuned. She played with me and read to me. She was down-to-earth, practical, creative and eager to help me learn life skills. But this strong attachment also set the stage for a fraught, stormy chapter when my adolescent drive toward separation and independence must have felt like yet another abandonment to her.

Having to grow up so quickly and independently, my father was an adult's adult, untutored in the ways of children. He had missed the first two years of my development and came home from the Army to a full-blown, stubborn, demanding, red-headed two-year-old who had no interest in sharing her mother. This must have been a shock to his system. He was

My mother and me in 1944.

not a patient man and could swear up a storm, particularly when defied by inanimate objects. After several clashes, I learned to fear his temper, read the highly nuanced signs of its advent and retreat to safety. In turn, he ceded the childrearing role to my mother. While usually laconic, he could talk up a storm with my mother and his buddies and could also engage in long rants when an issue riled him. These rants increased with age, frustration, and certainly with the presence of alcohol, with which he later struggled.

My mother's childhood etched two contradictory traits into her personality — enormous strength, intelligence and capability, juxtaposed with deep insecurity about her own worth, stemming, no doubt, from the successive abandonments by every major figure in her young life.

My mother and I lived in Las Cruces for two years while my father served in Europe. I have no memories of living in Las Cruces, but I loved my mother's stories of this period and made her tell them to me so often that I feel as though I remember them. My mother's youth and our Las Cruces years are captured in "My Mother's Story," a separate piece I wrote based on interviews with my mother (which is available to the interested reader).

Chapter ONE

Pre-Alaska: 1946 to 1950

Moving to Santa Fe

My father returned from the war in 1945. In a hurry to get his life on the road, he skipped finishing his degree and obtained a job as a draftsman with the New Mexico State Highway Department. Thus, when I was two, we moved from Las Cruces three hundred miles north to Santa Fe. We lived there until I was seven, after which we moved to Alaska. I have many distinct memories of people, places, and events in Santa Fe. Unfortunately, no one now alive shares these memories, since my parents are gone, my brother was only two when we left, and my sister had yet to be born. Nevertheless, they were formative years both for me and our young, financially struggling family. As a result, I have unusually strong feelings for Santa Fe, undoubtedly because it recalls my earliest bonds with my parents.

My mother tells me we initially rented a small, coal-heated house but the coal dust was ubiquitous and I was perpetually covered in it. For her, cleanliness was next to godliness, hard work, and self-sufficiency in the pantheon of family values, and so we rapidly moved.

Seton Village

Our second home was in "Seton Village" a small cluster of modest dwellings some seven miles south of Santa Fe owned by Ernest Thompson Seton, an upper-class British ex-patriot, naturalist, author, and co-founder of the Boy Scouts. He was famous for his nature books written for children. At my age, I did not find them interesting and, despite his seeming interest in children, I found him a cold and distant man. Perhaps it was a matter of social class — his being upper and ours being lower-middle at best.

Our Seton Village home consisted of a boxcar and a caboose, set on a high desert plain populated by cacti and tumbleweed. Living there was one step above camping, but just barely. Distinct images mark my memory of our time there: Primal terror, deeply instilled by my parents, as early one morning while sitting on the toilet, I watched a large snake creep up the bathroom door jamb. My parents' rescue and the safety and warmth of their bed as they cuddled and calmed me afterward. Walking on that high desert plain hand-in-hand with Dad. A train pulled by a steam locomotive far in the distance, chugging and puffing black cumulous clouds of smoke accompanied by an occasional, lonely train whistle. The quiet, the solitude, and the relentless wind. Coyotes howling at night. My mother making coffee in a coffee tin.

The high plain upon which Seton Village sat.

Other memories mark this earliest period. One was of having my tonsils removed — an overcrowded pediatric ward and my mother upset because my bed was jammed up against that of another child, sick with the flu. For me the high point of the episode was the unimagined luxury of eating as much jello and ice cream as I wanted. Also, the image of the steering wheel and car ceiling, the feeling of security as I lay across the front seat of our car, head in her lap, while my mother drove us home.

My mother took a job as a telephone operator for AT&T, while my father worked at the New Mexico State Highway Department. During this period, my mother acquired a modest inheritance from the sale of the family ranch. They discussed possibly buying a business — a laundry — but instead continued their jobs and decided to look for a house or land to purchase. Later in life, my mother claimed that this small nest egg was what put our family on our feet financially.

In our search, we visited one particularly deserted house in the windswept countryside west of Santa Fe. As they explored the house and the well, my parents commented on the prevalence of snakes, evoking anew my terror. Everything about the house bespoke dustiness, bleakness and abandonment. I found it scary and was relieved when they decided not to buy it.

Instead they purchased a piece of land in Tesuque, north of Santa Fe, where they could build their own house.

Living in Town (1945)

From Seton Village, my parents commuted the seven miles each way to Santa Fe, dropping me at daycare each morning. Tesuque is roughly ten miles on the opposite side of Santa Fe from Seton Village and, as they began to work evenings and weekends on our new house there, the commute became untenable and we moved to temporary quarters in Santa Fe, one of only two occasions when we

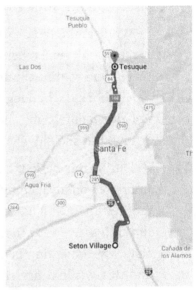

Map of Tesuque, Santa Fe, and Seton Village.

ever lived in a town or city. Both times, our stay was short and transitional. My parents were comfortable with living in the country, with our neighbors at a distance.

We rented the bottom-floor unit in a row of attached apartments owned by a family named Pick, who lived upstairs. They were Jewish and had a little girl my age. Come Christmas, my mother, who had no knowledge of the Jewish faith, was appalled at the thought that any child should wake up Christmas morning without a single present to open. So, she fixed the problem; she bought the little girl a Christmas gift.

While at the Picks', we had a small bulldog, whose name I don't remember. The children in the complex teased him continually and in response one afternoon after school, the bulldog bit a child. Tears and injustice notwithstanding, my mother got rid of it. She was strong, and she did what she had to do.

During this period, I saw my first movie, "Bambi." Imprinted on my memory is the rebuke by Thumper's mother upon finding Bambi's forest friends making fun of his awkward first attempts to walk— "If you can't say something nice, don't say anything at all," and this wisdom has served me well in life. Then I was devastated when the magnificent stag comes to the little fawn to announce that his mother has been killed by a hunter, and he will have to grow up brave and strong without her. (I later learned to skip the sad or scary movie parts by sudden rushes to the bathroom, predictably tipped off by ominous music). You can imagine my distress later that year when my father returned from a hunting expedition proudly displaying a large antelope tied over the hood of the car. For me, this was Bambi's mother.

Spoils of the antelope hunt. Dad on the left.

Labor Day each year kicks off "fiesta" in Santa Fe, in which the whole town participates. Fiesta begins at sundown Friday with a large procession pursuing Zozobra, dubbed "Old Man Gloom," a looming, 15-foot white effigy (since grown to 30 feet) made of white gauze over chicken wire stuffed with shredded paper. In their effort to banish sorrow, gloom and pain, the townspeople pursue, catch and burn the effigy. Bonfires of dry tumbleweed surround Zozobra, accompanied by fireworks, while his arms flail and he emits excruciating groans and cries, amplified by a megaphone. This event begins a weekend of merriment. I experienced it in a starkly different way, however. The flames were scary and I was beyond horrified thinking that someone was being burned to death. For me, fiesta was a Joan-of-Arc experience and it set the stage for a lifelong fear of fire. When we attended the following year, my mother was forced to extricate me quickly, as I screamed and cried, and that was our last fiesta.

Burning of Zozobra at the fiesta.

My mother read to me from the earliest days of my memory. Early on it was nursery rhymes, read from the first volume of *My Book House*. The volume was beloved and served all three of us children and my mother knew it so well she could recite it by heart. I would cuddle up on the couch with her after supper each night while she read. I loved these sessions, feeling warm, safe, and at one with her and the world. At the age of three we tackled my first chapter book — Louisa May Alcott's *Little Men* — reading a chapter each night. I did not understand it. But I so cherished the time with my mother that I hid my incomprehension, lest she give up reading to me altogether. When she finally discovered the truth, she exclaimed, "Why didn't you tell me?" She could not understand why I didn't speak up for myself, but I interpreted it as disappointment in me. I felt inadequate and terrible for letting her down.

I was a sentimental child. The Easter when I was three someone gave me a small, yellow, candy chick. I promptly fell in love him and played with him as you would a doll. After several days, however, my mother announced that he was getting stale and dirty and that I would either have to eat him or she would throw him away. My compromise was to eat one micro-bite-- about the size of a grain of sugar — each day. Alas, that strategy failed and one day I was forced to eat him, all in one despairing gulp.

Dinners in that period were prepared by my mother and father after we all arrived home at night. My generation is the last that will remember oleomargarine, which came in a white brick package and had to be mixed with yellow food coloring, at the behest of dairy farmers who feared competition. One evening I overheard my mother and father talking in the kitchen as they prepared dinner. They were clearly upset at something and my mother exclaimed in frustration, "Why don't we just shoot ourselves right now?!" I took this quite literally and lived, traumatized, with my heart in my throat for several days until perfect normalcy made clear there was no imminent threat. People should be careful what they say in front of children.

Tesuque (1946-1950)

Our property was located on Bishop Lodge Road in a small community called Tesuque (named after the nearby, famous Tesuque Pueblo). A stream, an everlasting source of cool relief, play, and fascination, ran behind our large backyard and through a small valley along the base of a hill, which loomed on the other side. An arroyo (dry creek bed) running beside our house at a right angle emptied into it. Unlike the high desert plain of Seton Village, the land around us, nurtured by the stream, was lush with cottonwood trees that populated the valley.

On the north side of our land was a horse farm, with horses that often came to socialize over the fence, fueling my youthful dream of becoming a cowboy. On the south side was an abandoned apple orchard that produced apples of otherworldly taste, which could be picked in abundance in the fall. Across the road was a regular farm worked by a family with five children who were my friends. Pumpkin was a year older than me and Marie a year younger. Besides dolls and cowboys, we loved playing in the stream together, building dams, lakes, villages, and boats. A herd of donkeys considered the valley their private property and were unimpressed by property lines, fences, gardens, the barking of Penny, our collie dog, or the scolding of my mother. Donkeys aren't dubbed stubborn for nothing. I cracked up at their braying, because they really do say "eeeee awhhhhh!"

Days were filled with work for my parents and daycare for me. Evenings and weekends were filled with building our new house. My parents were hard-working, and their mantra was that, if I couldn't help, at least I could stay out of their way, leaving me to my own ingenuity for entertainment. I can see them now, laying brick, pouring concrete and hauling large boulders in the wheel barrow to build the terrace. When they were in a good mood, I could catch a wheel-barrow ride as they returned for more boulders.

I mostly remember their breaks, however, when I could again relate to them. Sitting on the terrace, they once asked me to bring them a glass of water from the house, admonishing me to be careful lest I spill it. Earnestly obeying, I carried it slowly and carefully, grasping the glass with both hands, rim between my lips, to prevent it from spilling on its long journey. They laughed at my rigorous defense when it arrived nearly empty, but definitely unspilt, the loving laugh of parents enjoying their child's innocence and literal understanding. I can still see my mother, removing her shoes and wading in the stream, her answer for the fastest way to cool off on a hot day. Again, I see them both resting on a rock beside the stream, rolling cigarettes by pouring Bull Durham tobacco from a small, cloth, draw-string bag into small rectangles of tissue paper, rolling them and licking the edges to seal them.

Our house was built of cinder block but was spackled like adobe in the Spanish style. We moved in — or, more accurately, camped out — the moment it had four walls and a roof but before it had plumbing and a floor. For a brief period, a three-foot deep open trench ran through the spine of the house as my parents laid water and sewer lines. The arroyo beside the house filled with water only during flash floods, which occurred with some regularity. One night, a torrent of water careened through this ditch and thus through the middle of our house, separating me on one side and my parents on the other. I remained until my mother scooped me up in her arms and into safety.

Our house in Tesuque. The cottonwoods and arroyo beside, the hill behind.

Down the valley, past the apple orchard, a friend named Dooley bought land on the other side of the stream, requiring a bridge for access. My father, no doubt intrigued by the engineering involved, helped him build the bridge which came to be known, unsurprisingly, as "Dooley's Bridge." The bridge was downhill from

Ronda, age four, standing on Dooley's Bridge.

the road. One afternoon I played alone in our parked car while my parents worked on the bridge. Suddenly the car began to roll downhill. I've never seen my father move faster, catching up with the car, leaping into it and jamming on the brakes just as it threatened to head over the bridge and into the stream.

We often hiked up the large hill — to me a mountain — that loomed behind our house. It was sparsely populated with pinion trees, and in the summer, we scooped up handfuls of tiny, brown- and beige-streaked pinion nuts from beneath the trees, a free and delicious treat once tediously shelled. My parents, in a breathtaking act of faith (or foolishness), allowed me to hike the mountain by myself, after reinforcing in me the fear of snakes. One day following a storm, as I returned alone from the mountain and crossed Dooley's Bridge, I looked down to see a large snake in the water. It was nowhere near me but, remembering their words, I was terrified out-of-my-mind, convinced the world could end momentarily. I ran breathlessly all the way home, so filled with fear that upon arrival I vomited. My parents grabbed a shotgun and I led them back to find, of course, that the snake was already dead and floating in the water. They explained that it was harmless but, in my literal child's mind, a snake is a snake and the original instructions did not distinguish dead from alive.

As soon as our house was well along, we turned to building a large chicken coop in the back yard. Working on the roof was alluring and I begged to join my father. I was extraordinarily proud to be allowed climb the ladder and crawl onto the roof. Alas, however, I proved a disappointment. My father would start a row of nails for me to then hammer in. And, of course, every nail buckled under my clumsy, four-year-old aim, requiring that he pull them out and start again. This upset my father, who responded with curses. Fear, guilt, and inadequacy welled up in my chest. And then to compound matters, I discovered that climbing down was far scarier than climbing up. I froze in fear at the edge of the roof and had to be lifted down. Not an ego-building experience.

We regularly kept some two hundred chickens and sold their eggs, where and how I don't remember.

My job was to find and collect the eggs hidden in the straw of the chicken house — a bit like an Easter egg hunt — and to help in washing them and in feeding the chickens. Every few weeks we bought chicken feed — little army-green pellets slightly smaller than a pea — which was sold in large gunny sacks made of floral-print cotton fabric. I loved those trips since I got to choose the sack and, when it was empty, my mother made the cloth into blouses and dresses for me. Later she would make me clothes out of the remains of the bright red, blue, and yellow cotton fabric used by surveyors to flag their work (before they moved to plastic tape). We let nothing go to waste.

Beside the chicken house, my mother created a large garden. Baby tomato plants were incubated under glass in the ground and we grew cucumbers, radishes, lettuce, and onions. I had a love affair with watermelon. Impressed with seeing seeds turn into plants and then into vegetables, I asked to add watermelon seeds to my mother's garden. She explained that it wouldn't work; to grow, watermelons needed lots and lots of water. So instead I planted the seeds in the stream, with several rocks on top of them, designed to hold them down — from which never emerged any watermelons. The chicken coop remains on the property to this day.

Growing Pains

With few children around, my playmates became a motley band of dolls and stuffed animals — a red corduroy teddy bear, a small, stuffed oil-cloth elephant, and a hard rubber baby doll with moveable arm and hip joints; I considered these "my" family. One day, we found a doll on the road, no doubt dropped from the window of a passing car. I was thrilled. It was identical to my baby doll, albeit a bit worse for the wear, and now my "family" had twins, just like my cousins. And, while I never had a dollhouse, I played with a beloved miniature plastic doll family of four, each figure with moveable arm, hip and knee joints, and a set of miniature plastic dollhouse furniture. During this period, my mother bought me a small turtle with a painted shell. He played agreeably with my dollhouse family until one day he escaped and disappeared. We searched everywhere, and for nine days he was MIA. Just when we had given up finding him alive, he emerged from under the couch, apparently no worse for the wear, although later he lost his shell. Turtle shells should not be painted.

Sometime during this period, my father took flying lessons. For his last lesson, we were invited to join him in the Piper Cub in which he was training. Behold, below me unfolded the most exquisite miniature,

My father, Bill Stilley, taking flight lessons in 1947.

model village I could ever imagine — complete with houses; stores; streets; trees; real moving cars; and live people! I was overcome with excitement and my mother held me down lest I climb out the window to play. They laughed the way parents of young children do and tried to explain, but I wasn't buying it. I knew what I saw, and I was thrilled and then terribly disappointed by the inexplicable obstinacy of my parents. In retrospect, I am grateful that my father's interest in flying never progressed. Connoting the level of risk, private pilots are among the few uninsurable people, and few environments are riskier than where we ended up in Alaska.

I loved my tricycle. It was my horse (when I wasn't riding my broom, which sufficed as a hobby horse), my bike, and my car. I could only play with it in the house and on the sidewalk my father had built in front of the house, but in my imagination, it took me everywhere. Upside down, it became an engine, with its flywheel driven by the pedals, and I was the mechanic. I also remember my excitement when we discovered the offer of three dolls — named Snap, Crackle, and Pop — on the back of Rice Krispies box. We sent away for them and what disappointment when they arrived: cheap, stuffed fabric with painted-on doll features.

A better companion was our beloved dog Penny, a full-blooded, rust-and-white collie — the image of Lassie. Gentle, loyal, and smart, Penny could be counted on to hang out with me as I roamed the backyard, played in the stream, climbed the mountain or played around the house. She didn't mind joining my doll family but did not take well to playing dress-up. A beautiful dog, she was stolen three times (my parents blamed "the Mexicans") and each time, several days later, she would return tired, dirty, and disheveled, to an amazed and joyous household, obviously having escaped and travelled no one knows how many miles. When we left for Alaska, Penny went to live with my aunt and uncle and cousins in Las Cruces.

I spent hours walking around the backyard, making up stories to entertain myself — usually cowboy stories of which I was, of course, the child hero. I desperately wanted to be a cowboy and I wanted all the accoutrements that go with it — cowboy hat, chaps, bolero, and especially cowboy boots and spurs. I won on the hat, but lost on the chaps, boots, and spurs. I had a rope, but endless hours of practice never revealed the secrets of the lasso. Every adult I met implored me to be a cowgirl and nothing made me more indignant. I couldn't imagine anything stupider than wearing a skirt and sitting sideways on a horse. Why did anyone think I would settle for such a distant second-best? Instead I did the best I could, wearing my jeans, tucking my hair up into my cowboy hat, and pretending to be a boy. From early on I knew that a girl was viewed as being second best.

Dress-up was another favorite pastime of this period. Two of my dad's army uniforms with a series of ribbons on the jacket breast hung in my parents' closet for years. As a young child, I asked him what the ribbons were for. He replied, "You get them for brushing your teeth." Though mystified, I earnestly believed his answer for several years.

During this period, my grandfather came to visit for the first and only time (my father was estranged from his family). He was a doting grandfather, totally smitten with me and therefore I with him. He spent time with me, read to me, was interested in me and was always full of admiration. My parents loved me dearly, but doting had never been on the agenda. My mother had taught me simple embroidery and I gave him one of my hand-embroidered handkerchiefs. He was over the moon with it, and it secured me forever in his eyes as a child prodigy. How thrilled I was when, hearing of my longing for cowboy boots, he agreed to buy them for me! Then my mother found out. No cowboy boots.

The bane of my childhood was my lazy right eye, so noticeable that I have worn glasses from the age of two and was the only child I knew wearing glasses until I was joined by Pinky Johnson in the third grade. By four, however, the doctor recommended a patch over my good eye, to be worn half a day for two years. Oh, how I despised it! I can still smell the old-fashioned white adhesive tape today and feel it first sticking to my face then being pulled off. Not only did I stumble around half blind, seeing only through my poor eye but, far worse, strangers would rush up to me asking with alarm what happened. I felt like an imposter, having to tell them that exactly nothing happened! Why couldn't they just go away and leave me alone? I would have far preferred teasing to pity.

We were now commuting from Tesuque to Santa Fe, my parents to work and me to nursery school. Every morning, my mother served fried eggs with hard yolks for breakfast. I had an aversion to fried eggs, but she was strict about our eating what was put in front of us and I knew I didn't stand a chance in an outright showdown with her. So, I turned to subterfuge. Somewhere I acquired the notion that it was more palatable to store the egg in the side of my cheek than to gulp it down.

To compound matters, a neighbor joined us for the commute — a large, affable, overbearing man named McDonald. I would sit squeezed in the front seat between my two parents and McDonald would breathe down my neck as he leaned forward from the back seat to talk to them. His regular breakfast fare seemed to involve large quantities of garlic. Thus, I would sit, despised fried egg in cheek, withering under his garlic breath, my parents both smoking, for the half hour it took to get to my nursery school where, at last, I could flee the car and run to the nearest garbage can to spit out the egg. The day finally came, however, when I was discovered. Rather than being angry, as I had expected, my mother backed off, clearly impressed with the strength of my will, if not of my aversion. Mercifully, that was the last time I had to eat fried eggs for breakfast. I still don't like fried eggs with hard yolks (but garlic is okay, if it's on my breath and not someone else's).

Besides fried eggs, I utterly despised canned tomatoes, which my mother served regularly as a vegetable for dinner. But she knew no mercy and, despite my many pleas, I was forced to eat them. I don't know why she was such a hard-liner. Maybe because she had been hungry at times in her life or, in her dislike of cooking, maybe she wanted to make clear that serving more than one meal was not in the plan.

One afternoon I was walking around our backyard thinking and talking to myself when I stumbled upon something I didn't understand: My mother was a very nice person, but why was she so mean when it came to canned tomatoes? Then a revelation came to me. Being a nice person, if she knew what canned tomatoes tasted like to me, she surely wouldn't make me eat them. To her they probably tasted like chocolate ice cream, I mused. But then I quickly realized that there would be no way that she, or anyone else for that matter, could ever know how awful they tasted to me. My five-year-old mind had just discovered the concept of subjectivity. A few years later my little brother (yet to be born) disliked some other food; he and I created a united front to make our case, and my mother relented.

The new rule allowed us each to choose one food, and one food only, that we could pass up when served. My choice was canned tomatoes. I don't remember my brother's. Now we had stumbled onto the concept of strength in unity.

Leisure

Despite my parents' hard work and sacrifice, we also had fun. Occasionally we went to a movie, at either at a movie house or a drive-in. Movie houses then had enclosed seating for families with small children, and when my brother was an infant, my parents let me sit outside, right in front of them, by myself. I soon discovered that I could leave, unnoticed in the dark, and sit in the front row, which I thought was prime seating. Several movies later, my parents discovered me missing and panicked and that was the end of that. I would fall asleep in the back seat of the car on the way home and my father would carry me into the house and tuck me in. I so liked his strong arms and tenderness that, on nights when I didn't fall asleep, I faked it. I remember one night as we returned home, we saw a flash flood in the headlights of our car, as it roared down the dry creek bed beside Bishop Lodge road. We outraced it home just in time to see it come tearing down the arroyo beside our house.

A Sunday get-away often consisted of going for a drive. Air conditioning did not yet exist and, during the hot summer, the air, blowing in through the open car windows, cooled us. Very occasionally the drive included a special treat — an ice cream cone. The round cones came to an alluring point and my mother warned me many times not to bite off the tip. On one occasion, however, I was overcome with temptation and bit it off anyway. Cream streamed down my face, hands, arms, and shirt. My mother fumed. I begged her not to throw it away, and she relented. I never bit off the tip of another ice cream cone.

My father enjoyed the company of his buddies, most of whom were work colleagues. In addition to hunting, he went rafting down the Rio Grande River. We dropped him off upstream and then picked him up downstream three days later. He had spent much of the trip barefoot in the boat, and he had third-degree burns on the tops of his feet. We took him directly from the boat to the doctor.

My mother had friends who occasionally got together, perhaps to play cards. I think most were from her office. One Saturday, the get-together took place at our house and for the occasion my mother baked two lemon meringue pies, an all-time favorite of mine. Her meeting had no place for children. She had told me beforehand to be good, not interrupt their meeting, and meanwhile I could have as much lemon meringue pie as I wanted. I hung out in the kitchen, bored with the whole endless event. I was very good, however, and took her at her word, eating first one piece of pie and then another. When the meeting ended, and refreshment time came, however, only one pie remained. Her friends were both amazed and amused, marveling in my seemingly bottomless capacity for lemon meringue pie. I fiercely defended myself, reciting her instructions, and she did not get angry. She was a very fair person.

A Baby Brother Is Born (1948)

My brother was born when I was five. My parents aroused me from my sleep in the middle of the night, and we drove to town in the darkness. My father parked on the street beside the hospital where I was left to sleep in the locked car while they disappeared inside. I didn't sleep much that night and the hours ticked by very slowly. Shortly after daybreak I got out to play on the sidewalk when my father appeared exuberantly announcing the arrival of my new baby brother, Alan. He was happier than I had ever seen him.

To celebrate, he took me out to a restaurant for breakfast, an unprecedented event. Magnanimously, he offered anything I wanted for breakfast. "Anything I wanted?" I confirmed. Delighted, I proceeded to order mushroom soup, one of my favorite foods (second only to egg custard and lemon meringue pie). The waiter was taken back as was my father. Clearly, neither had anticipated my choice. Then my father set about convincing me to make a more conventional choice, whereupon I learned that adults don't always mean exactly what they say. Freedom of choice notwithstanding, I was honored to be taken out to breakfast by my dad.

The arrival of my brother changed many things. First, my mother stayed home for most of the year, a first in my memory. My father had badly, badly wanted a boy and Alan fulfilled that dream. His name, Alan Neil, was a tribute to a man in Colorado who had befriended and mentored my father after he left home. My brother would have been named "Alan Hill," except for my mother's veto. "Neil" was a close as my father could get. Alan's birth gave Dad his first opportunity to bond and experience a baby from the moment of birth. My father did not mean badly, but his preference for Alan was overt and periodically throughout early childhood left me feeling helplessly crushed under an inadequacy I was powerless to address.

Childcare

I had a variety of childcare arrangements during these years. I do not remember in what order they occurred, but my favorite was Pauline, the cousin of my mother's colleague, Lucy. She was kind, of Mexican background, and she made the best sopapillas in the world. For a period, she also cared for a little boy, Michael, whom I liked. She lived across the street from a funeral parlor and our favorite game, as we played in the dirt of her yard with our little cars and dolls, was "funeral home." My mother was certain that if outsiders ever found out, they would judge us morbid if not mentally ill. Michael and I pledged to get married and we didn't understand the adults' response. A boy and a girl who liked each other — what else do you need? Isn't that how it works? Pauline hung her wash on lines beside her house to dry. One day, Michael and I were making mud pies. Pauline's beautiful white sheets were billowing in the wind and the temptation to see our handprints on those sheets overcame us. I had never seen a human being more livid than Pauline was. I was terrified. She blamed Michael, who I think was probably the instigator. I wasn't quite bold enough myself.

Other childcare arrangements were austere by comparison. There were nursery schools, the first run by Mrs. Wiswald and the second by Mrs. Parsons. They were largely custodial, preceding any notion of child development or learning. Life at Mrs. Parsons's was strict, boring, and bleak. She was mean. There were few toys and no organized activities aside from strictly enforced lunch and naps. I had no friends, no one to talk to. For hours, I would stand alone in the one corner of the yard where, through a chain-link fence, I could see my mother leave in the morning and return in the evening. And in between, that post also allowed me to watch trains slowly traversing back and forth over a railroad trestle spanning the street a half block away.

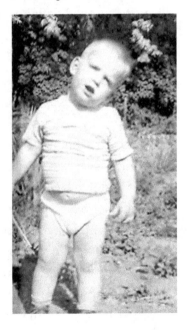

For a brief period after my brother was born, I was cared for by his babysitter, Mrs. Valdez. Their family lived on a farm on the outskirts of town, and I loved sailing "boats" in the **Alan, age two, at Mrs. Valdez.'**

irrigation ditches that surrounded each field. One day, I accompanied the Valdez family on a trip. Mr. Valdez was extremely proud of his car. In the backseat, however, I accidentally spilled water. Threatening to tattle on me, their daughter, a few years older, terrorized me the entire day by telling me that, when he found out, her father would whip me. What a miserable day! Clearly, no such thing happened and, at the end of the day when my mother arrived, I at last exhaled. I wasn't so eager to return to Mrs. Valdez the next day, and I definitely steered clear of her daughter.

School

Kindergarten did not exist in 1948 and, when I reached school age, Alan and I commuted into Santa Fe with my parents, he to go to Mrs. Valdez and me to attend school. My mother vowed that her children would never attend a one-room school house — all that Tesuque had to offer. Woods Gormley Elementary School in Santa Fe was three blocks from the State Capitol Building where my father worked. After school, I would walk by myself the three, tree-lined blocks to his building and play on the grounds until he got off work at 5:00 p.m. A tall, stately pine tree stood in front of the building with boughs so long, low, and thick that it formed a cavern at the base of

Woods-Gormley School, photo taken in 1984.

the trunk. This became my afternoon fort, den, and playhouse. Occasionally, Dad or his co-workers would come to check on me and, at five o'clock, he and I would pile into the car and go to pick up my mother and brother.

My first-grade teacher, Mrs. Mendenhall, was a very strict woman, given quickly to anger and corporal punishment. The first day of school she asked how many children could read. I interpreted this to mean that I should already know how to read and that I was already behind. I was flabbergasted. This was exactly what I had waited so long for and the very reason I had come to school! That year, in addition to reading, I learned right from left. For the Pledge of Allegiance each morning, we were instructed to stand beside our desks and put our right hand on our heart. My right hand was nearest my desk. Being a bit dyslexic, I've always remembered my right hand by visualizing myself standing next to my first-grade desk.

I only got in trouble once that year, and that was for exuberantly holding hands with the little girl across the aisle from me. I think her name was Lois. Mrs. Mendenhall dragged us both to the front of the room where she lined us up to smack our hands with a yardstick for the benefit of all to see and learn. By the end of first grade, I was increasingly discovering the benefits of invisibility.

Winters were cold in Santa Fe and one day at recess I slipped on the ice at school and fell on my wrist. The pain was excruciating, so bad that I could barely move my hand, but it did not outweigh my aversion to telling anyone — a dislike of others fussing over me and a childish fear that the cure would prove worse than the malady. Two days later my parents discovered the injury, which we assumed to be a sprain, and my mother bound it until the pain went away.

Moving to Alaska (1950)

My parents came to feel uncomfortable in Santa Fe. My father had been working as a draftsman for

Ronda and Alan, ages six and one.

the Highway Department for five years, and with a gubernatorial election came the threat of losing his job. Opportunity was one issue, crime another. One night, driving home in the dark after working late, he came to a roadblock on the deserted, two-lane Bishop's Lodge Road. Quick wits and driving skill prevented him from being held up, but the incident shook my parents. Rightly or wrongly, they felt that Mexicans were the majority population, controlled the machinery of government in Santa Fe, and discriminated against "Anglos."

My father received a job offer as a full-blown engineer for the federal Bureau of Public Roads in Juneau, Alaska, which was then a US territory. The position was a significant promotion and came with enhanced pay because of Alaska's status as a "hardship" post. Moreover, my parents had no roots holding them to New Mexico. The obligation was for two years and they figured that, if they didn't like it, they could always transfer elsewhere. So, they decided to move. Having few friends, no love of Woods Gormley, and no idea of what a move meant, I had no fears or regrets about leaving — except when it came to the loss of our dog, Penny, whom I dearly loved, and a good many of my toys. For many years, the peculiar appearance of my sled commemorated the move. Its steering bar had to be trimmed on both sides to fit the packing crate, but this didn't prevent it from being the fastest sled and an object of admiration in my future neighborhood.

My parents had received an offer on our house and were packing with just enough time to reach Alaska when the house sale fell through. My father felt forced to proceed alone to begin work, while leaving my mother behind to sell the house and follow. I have nothing but admiration for her strength. She continued to work full time, manage the logistics of two small children, sell the house and pack and ship our belongings before driving, by herself, with those two small children, more than one thousand miles to Seattle. I heard no complaints and I knew that my role was to help and not demand. We sold the house to Austin "Slim" Green, a maker of customized celebrity saddles. He subsequently enlarged the house, added a basement workshop and lived there for over 50 years, making saddles for Gene Autry and other Western notables. As an adult, I returned a few times and was impressed with how small the place looked in comparison to my memories. I'm sure that images are remembered in inverse proportion to body size.

We travelled by car and our trip took place in August 1950, prior to the existence of interstate highways. On the road, we would awake at 5:30 each morning, when it was still cool, drive until mid-afternoon, find a motel and a playground, stop for the day and unwind. One day in Utah, a car full of rowdy young men stalked us. They would pull up to our tailgate, pass, and then slow to a crawl in front of us, forcing us to pass or, worse, stop. Then they would begin all over again, hooting, laughing, and yelling the whole time. We were scared for our lives. That day we stopped early in a small town. As we pulled aside, I still remember their laughter as they sped by us. We spent the rest of the day looking over our shoulders to make sure they were not coming back. The day was torridly hot, and we found not only a motel, but a playground with a sprinkler. Only in the rapture of the cool spray did the white-hot hand of fear release its grip.

Every morning Alan, two years old, woke up starved. He loved "hot cakes" and from the moment we entered a restaurant he would scream "Hot cakes! Hot cakes! Hot cakes!" at the top of his lungs, until he was finally served. We couldn't pretend we did not know him but instead apologized our way from Santa Fe to Seattle.

In Seattle, we were to catch the *Aleutian*, one of two steamships then servicing Southeastern Alaska, for the three-day trip to Juneau. Arriving, however, we discovered that some mix-up would cause us a week's delay in our departure. We went from motel to motel, finding them all filled, and reminding us of the plight of Joseph and Mary. At last we found an inexpensive motel, which had just reopened after a flood. It was far from downtown and from there we explored a city bigger than I could ever imagine. I visited my first department store and rode my first escalator, at one point finding my mother doubled over in laughter as I desperately ran up the down escalator to reach her on the second floor.

S.S. Aleutian, 1950s.

(Alaska State Library, Skinner Foundation Photo Collection)

Finally, the day for boarding the ship came. I was very excited. Our stateroom was several levels below deck. Once we arrived and deposited our luggage, I was eager to go back up on the deck, so I could see the ship depart. I was certain I knew the way. Upon deciding to return to my mother, however, I found that suddenly every deck, staircase, and stateroom door looked alike. Running up and down, back and forth, I began to panic. Meanwhile, my mother, thinking I had been gone too long, began looking for me and similarly panicked. She marshalled the stewards to look for an unaccompanied freckle-faced, red-headed, seven-year-old girl; one of them finally found me. After we departed, she told me that she had been ready to get off the boat, thinking that was what I had done.

Chapter

Living on Lake Creek: 1950 to 1953

Arriving in Juneau

My most salient memory of arriving in Juneau in 1950 was the smell of the steamship docks — a combination of wood, creosote, sea water, and the sulfurous odor

Juneau, Alaska in the 1950s.

of mudflats that to this day evokes instant recognition and nostalgia. At that time, Juneau, a town of 10,000 (counting environs), inhabited a small wedge of land, squeezed tightly between the waterfront of Gastineau Channel and two enormous, looming mountains — Mt. Juneau and Mt. Roberts. The waterfront was lined with docks, a cold storage plant, a seaplane port, a decommissioned submarine port, mudflats, and the boat harbor. A small business district paralleled the waterfront. Stores, offices, and schools climbed the steep slope and eventually gave way to homes clinging to the mountainsides. The incline was so steep that the front door of my first elementary school was located up a set of steps from Fifth Street and the back door exited three floors above, across a ramp onto Sixth Street. Toward the upper edges of the town, streets gave way to steep wooden stairways, and persistent precipitation often threatened these neighborhoods with mud or snow slides. To the south, the biggest structure of all — the abandoned Alaska Juneau mine, with its long, horizontal, multi-story sheet metal buildings with red tin roofs — clutched the side of Mt. Roberts. Except for Honolulu, Juneau is the only state capitol inaccessible by road from the mainland.

Snowy weather made the steep streets of Juneau harrowing on foot or by car. In the winter, when the sky cleared, temperatures plummeted into the negative numbers and the "Taku Winds" would gust down at 60 to 80 mph from the ice cap, the large, solid mass of ice which engulfs the upper reaches of the coastal range and from which the glaciers flow, sending Juneau-ites running for cover or clinging to the nearest stationary object. One snowy evening our family was headed to the hospital, located on Sixth Street, to visit a friend. With great momentum and the car in low gear, my father headed up steep, icy Main Street. As he moved to turn onto Sixth Street, the car lost momentum, skidded, did a one-eighty and we continued our trip, but downhill. With our hearts in our throats, no one uttered a word until, at the bottom, we finally exhaled and laughed at such a perfect, if undesired, maneuver. Although the place was chronically rainy most of the year, no one I knew owned or used an umbrella, a fact I did not notice until I went south to college in Oregon. Wondering why, upon return, I noticed that the downtown businesses had all built attached overhangs, allowing pedestrians to walk around downtown unimpeded by the rain. They were so commonplace that I had failed to notice them.

When our ship docked, my father was waiting for us on the dock and our reunion was joyous. My mother, having risen to the many solitary challenges of our move, breathed a sigh of relief now that she once more had a partner with whom to share the responsibilities. Several blocks away, Dad had rented a temporary apartment in a large wood-frame house on Willoughby Avenue until we could get ourselves situated and purchase a home. One of four apartments, it was a dreary, dark, wall-papered efficiency on the second floor with two double beds, one for my brother and me, the other for my parents. Willoughby was a run-down street that paralleled Gastineau Channel. At one end was a boat shop, sub-port, and the business district, and at the other end was the ramshackle Native Village, so designated by the Bureau of Indian Affairs.

Houses on our side of the street sat on pilings encrusted below with seaweed, barnacles, and mussels. The smell of the mudflats wafted up as tides came and went. Only a few feet separated these houses. A massive bluff with a lengthy set of wooden steps stood between Willoughby, the shore and the flats below, and the town above us, including the Federal Office Building where my father worked. Every day I was allowed to climb the steps by myself to meet him when he got off for lunch and at the end of the day. I would wait in the grand and cavernous, if dreary, marble lobby, peering through the doors into the dark and empty elevator shafts to watch as the mysterious ropes and pulleys, accompanied by groans and whirrs, delivered the elevator cabs and eventually my dad out of the darkness. I loved walking home holding his hand.

In the house next door to us on Willoughby Avenue lived an African-American family, one of the very few in Juneau. As we left our apartment one day, my mother used the n-word in referring to the family, just as our neighbor happened to emerge from her house. Hearing it, she went ballistic, loudly chewing my mother up one side and down the other. My mother was stunned and mortified. She was a product of her times and had no exposure to African-Americans. She had no idea that she was giving offense. That was just the language people around her used. None of us ever forgot that.

Fires were a life-threatening danger in Juneau, given cold temperatures, high winds, overheated oil- and wood-fueled stoves, and wood-frame buildings. They were announced by ominous, two-tone blasts of a fire siren, loud enough to be heard throughout the whole town, the sequence of which — in its own Morse code — announced the fire's location. When the siren sounded, all activity in Juneau stopped while everyone young and old held their breath, hearts in their throats while they listened, counted, and calculated the whereabouts of the fire. Juneau was so small that, if it wasn't your own home or street, you usually knew

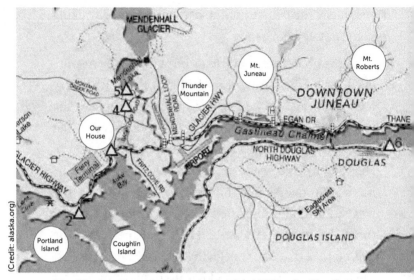

(Credit: alaska.org)

A modern era map of Juneau. In the 1950s, the North Douglas Highway did not exist.

whose it was. Everyone knew someone who had been burned out. It was highly personal.

We parked our car on Willoughby Avenue for that month. During the third week, the boat shop, five doors down, caught fire. Between the many paints and solvents and the wood-frame building, it went up like a matchstick, with flames shooting five stories into the air. Everyone came out onto the street to watch. The roar was deafening. Heat radiated off my face and terror welled up in my chest. Should the wind change, the fire could easily rip down the street, taking all those closely spaced, wood-frame buildings with it, including ours.

At one point, my mother instructed me to run upstairs to our apartment and fetch the car keys, in case the fire spread and we needed to evacuate quickly. With my heart in my throat, I ran upstairs and looked high and low, but no keys. The more I looked, the more desperate I grew, expecting the fire to swoop down at any moment to incinerate us all. And it would all be my fault because I could not find the car keys. I was in a state of hysteria by the time my mother appeared to tell me that she had been mistaken after all and had found the keys in her purse.

The memory of the heat on my face and that unique, acrid smell of burning buildings are as vivid today as it was then. That smell and any sound like that nightmarish siren still have the power to throw me into panic. I was so frightened of fires that for several years afterward, I would sneak out into our yard, particularly on nights when the wind would suck the fire from our oil-fired space heater up into the flue and stovepipe, looking up to our chimney and roof to assure myself that our house was not afire. My parents never knew.

Auke Bay

My parents soon found property to buy in Auke Bay, a wilderness community of barely two hundred people, fifteen miles north of Juneau, named for its original

DeHart's Store, Auke Bay, 1950s.

inhabitants, a subgroup of the Tlingit people called the Aak'w K̲wáan. The population then was sparse and spread out, the conditions pioneering. Typical of the population were the occupations of my friends' fathers — fisherman, carpenter, longshoreman, sheet metal worker, airplane mechanic, and ice man (who retrieved icebergs from the glacier lake, cut them into blocks, and sold them to households still using ice boxes). I knew that my father's status as an engineer with a government job made us better off than my friends' families, but the challenge of survival on the frontier was the ultimate equalizer.

At that time the roads in Auke Bay were unpaved. There were no phones and certainly no water, sewer, public transportation services, or postal delivery. We did have electricity, however, thanks to the Depression-era Rural Electrification Association (called, "the REA" or "the Coop"). Later Auke Bay developed a volunteer fire department. The heart of the community consisted of two small general stores — DeHart's and Taylor's — located about a half mile apart on the bay. Both sold groceries, gas, bait, and liquor, and both maintained their own docks and floats for mooring boats. Taylor's also housed the post office. In between was Horton's — a small, dark, ill-stocked, dust-laden hardware store. We lived about a mile from the bay on "Loop Road," which led to Mendenhall Glacier, circumnavigated Glacier Valley in front of it, and provided an alternate, longer, and more remote route for getting to Juneau. In common parlance, we all lived "out the road."

My folks purchased a small, red, frame house with a window-enclosed sunporch, set in a clearing back a good distance from the road. Alaska spruce and hemlock loomed around us. Dense underbrush engulfed every clearing and snuggled up to the house. Lake Creek, a sizable stream, ran beside it and then under the road and down to Auke Lake, a quarter-mile away.

In August, dark red, densely-packed salmon filled Lake Creek. Cars would stop on the bridge to watch the fish and I was frequently horrified to see children throwing rocks attempting to hit them. Upon spawning,

Our first house, garage and chicken coop on Lake Creek in Auke Bay. The creek runs between the buildings.

the fish would die, and rotting carcasses would bathe our house and yard with an unbearable stench. Every few days we would all don knee boots, pick up rakes, hoes or shovels, and haul the carcasses down-stream, away from our house. Dead fish also dampened the joy of playing in the creek during late summer and gave birth to a family expression that any odiferous person, food or object "smells like old dead fish." Across the creek from our house on a grassy field sat our large, red chicken house in which we kept two hundred Rhode

Island Red chickens. We sold eggs, introducing brown eggs to the Juneau market for the first time.

Mom Goes to Work

A few days after we arrived, Bill Norton, Director of the Rural Electrification Association (REA, or "the Coop") stopped at our house on his monthly meter-reading rounds. After a friendly chat, he mentioned that he had lost his bookkeeper. Did my mother have experience and was she interested? I admired her spunk. She had clerical but not bookkeeping experience, but she easily convinced herself and him that she could do it and she readily learned on the job, where she remained for six years. Later she took correspondence courses toward getting a CPA.

That fall, Alan, age three, went to our neighbor, Mrs. Reddekopp, for childcare, I went to school, and my mother began work. The REA was staffed by three people: Bill Norton, the director, John Simonstead, the linesman, and my mother, working half time. Headquarters was a small, one-room, white wood shack on the waterfront by the public dock, filled mostly with large wooden spools of electric line, transformers, tools, barrels of creosote, and other line equipment. My mother's bookkeeping operation consisted of an adding machine, a typewriter, a ledger, and some files — but no phone — and inhabited a small space at one end of the building. Despite the cold, the shack was not insulated and had no plumbing, with staff relying instead on an outhouse in the woods. When she arrived in the wintertime, my mother's first job was shoveling snow from the steps and starting a fire to thaw frost off both the line and office equipment. She worked from 8:00 a.m. to noon. In the summers, I stayed by myself, although in our first summer, babysitting arrangements for my brother fell through and I "took care" of him. I was eight and he was three. God takes care of fools and children and, I'm not sure who was who, but we managed to survive. In mid-morning, Alan and I would leave home, walk the mile to my mother's office on the Bay, and hang out until my mother got off work.

While waiting, my favorite activity was fishing off the public float, which my mother could see from her office window. The waters were filled with fish — tom cod, rock cod, flounder, bullfish, jellyfish, to name a few, and the mystery of what would come up loomed with every tug on the line. Most were not considered edible. Although I acquired a rod and reel, many children used a short piece of a broom handle, around which they wound their fishing line. Virtually anything would do as bait. Often, we would catch a fish, carve

Alan, age three and me, age eight with our "catch".

it into pieces and use those. Other times, a ripe berry or even a leaf would do. The hook barely needed to hit the water to get a bite. When noon came, we would walk home with my mother. She tells of an occasion when a whale swam into the bay. She walked down on the float to see it just yards away and reported being overwhelmed by the stench of its bad breath as it spouted. Definitely "old dead fish."

When we moved into our house, we inherited a white mother cat whose name I don't recall, two white kittens named Nip and Tuck and a black cocker spaniel named Butch, the most stubborn dog on earth. Every few months, Butch's hair would grow long, dirty and matted and my mother would grab the shears and give him a haircut. He would then cower under the table for hours, too embarrassed to come out. During our first earthquake, as the house shook and groaned, we had no idea what was happening. My mother suddenly had a revelation. Butch was scratching himself under the table causing the house to shake! We never let her forget it and long after he was dead, when we felt a tremor, we would announce that Butch was scratching himself.

We were not cat people. The mother cat and Nip figured this out quickly and wisely sought refuge elsewhere. Tuck, stubborn soul that he was, however, stuck around, seemingly to spite us. In our first year, my mother planted a large garden where she proudly raised cabbages, onions, radishes, carrots, swiss chard, and lettuce. That summer she caught Tuck spraying her cabbages and that was it. His jig was up. Simultaneously, my father met a small crew of researchers who were living and working up on the ice field above Juneau. Their camp was plagued by a woodchuck who lived under their quarters. Great minds leapt to the same the solution and that was Tuck. So, Tuck went to live on the ice cap. At last word, the researchers reported that Tuck had found common cause with the woodchuck and they had moved in together. Totally in character. That's the last we heard of Tuck.

Houses were far apart, rarely within sight of each other. Except for the Weidners, the family living across the road, our nearest neighbors were easily a mile away and most women were home all day without cars. My father and Hal Weidner decided we needed an emergency communications system. Hal was an electrical engineer and communications expert. Together, they purchased army surplus phone sets — heavy gray metal boxes about a foot square with an in-laid crank and a receiver — and laid the telephone lines themselves. The system served five families and calls were initiated by cranking the box according to the number and sequence of rings (buzzes) assigned to the family you wanted to reach. It worked, but since the lines lay on the ground, it was never reliable. We didn't get real phones until my last year of high school.

Frugality
Our family, starting out with so little, was frugal and endlessly ingenious in saving money.

There being no garbage pick-up, every couple of weeks we hauled our own garbage to the public dump at Tee Harbor. The dump served as an anonymous swap meet. People would leave usable items in plain view for others to take. Occasionally we would see others using our castaways and I'm sure they often saw us doing the same with theirs.

Purchased foods were expensive so we took pride in maximizing every natural, free, or cheap source of food — gardening, berry-picking, canning, hunting, fishing, raising chickens. In this vein, my father and Hal Weidner decided to try making their own home brew. An unpleasant brown liquid filled large crocks, and even our bathtub, until it was eventually poured into bottles, capped, and put away to ferment. Ours were stored in our wellhouse, theirs in their garage. One evening several weeks later we heard a "pow" coming from the wellhouse, followed by another and another. The aging bottles of brew had become grenades, exploding one by one, showering glass and beer throughout the interior of the wellhouse. We called the Weidners on our army surplus phone, who quickly discovered the same mortar fire taking place in their garage. After that, my Dad just bought his beer.

Because other consumer goods were expensive and frequently unavailable in Juneau, we ordered everything possible from Sears Roebuck or Montgomery Ward, which were located "stateside." Twice a year we eagerly awaited the new catalogue, the size of a doorstop, in which every conceivable consumer good was pictured and described — clothes, shoes and boots, toys, kitchen and bathroom goods, linen, household equipment and furniture, bicycles, sports goods, tools, yard equipment, cameras. We spent incalculable hours poring wishfully over the pages, our version of window-shopping, and, by the time the next catalogue arrived, our favorite pages would be food-stained, dog-eared, and tattered. For me, highlights were shoes, boots, coats, toys, dolls and bicycles and then later, cameras. For my mother, it was fabrics, household goods, and kitchen equipment. Ordering, however, was an exercise in delayed gratification. Relying on two steamships a week, the order, once mailed, would take at least a week to reach its stateside destination and, once fulfilled, another two weeks for the goods to arrive back in Auke Bay. And that was on a good day. Then, heaven forbid if the item had to be returned or exchanged.

We sewed all the clothing we possibly could for ourselves, leaving us dependent on the catalogue for shoes, boots, underwear, outerwear, and my Dad's clothing. Every woman sewed, and I learned around the age of eleven. While I became proficient, I harbor the worst disposition for a seamstress — a combination of impatience and perfectionism — so I can say that I do not really enjoy it. I remember our neighbor, Mrs. Howerter, mother of five children and an excellent seamstress, making her elementary school daughter, Ivagene, a graduation dress. Ivagene protested plaintively, "But I want a new dress." Her mother replied, "But I am making you a new dress." Ivagene resisted emphatically, "No, Mommy. I mean *new*." New meant store-bought.

My mother ordered essentials in bulk. My brother and I briefly liked shredded wheat for breakfast, so my mother ordered a carton of some twenty boxes. To her chagrin, Alan and I, in short order, lost our appetites for shredded wheat, leaving eighteen boxes still to be consumed. Bulk orders included canned goods, powdered milk, Velveeta cheese, and a thick, orange-colored concentrate which came in a gallon-sized glass jug and, when diluted, bore a vague resemblance to orange juice. My mother ordered evaporated milk by the carton until the day she died. More than once we obtained odd lots of damaged food whose origin I do not know — once a crate of cheese came with one end chewed by mice. We simply cut off the chewed-on parts and ate the rest.

Outside of the vegetables we grew, we considered fresh produce, with few exceptions, unaffordable. We ate canned vegetables and fruit, which were largely devoid of color and taste, if not nutrition. When, in my adolescence, the frozen versions began to appear on store shelves, my father disliked them, proclaiming that they were "undercooked." To this day, I will still eat fruit that is just short of rotten.

Juneau was serviced by three dairies, but we considered fresh milk a luxury, so we used powdered milk, attempting to camouflage its watery texture by adding evaporated milk. Butter and cream cheese were luxury items, which I did not experience until leaving Alaska. I give credit to my mother for her nutritional good sense, limited as it was by the information available at the time. She always insisted on three meals a day, with dinner a family sit-down. Dinner always consisted of a protein, a vegetable, and a starch, accompanied by biscuits or muffins — often my job — or white bread. These were customarily bathed in white gravy made of flour, drippings, and evaporated milk — also my job. We had no idea about saturated fat, so we conserved bacon grease and other drippings for cooking. I later learned that a favorite dish which we frequently made was called "chicken-fried steak," an inexpensive piece of steak, striated, dipped in flour, and pan fried in copious bacon drippings. "Licking the pan" was the best part. The very worst was spam, similarly floured and fried in bacon grease — only slightly better if baked and slathered in mustard sauce.

I smile at my mother. Although the variety was very basic and limited, when it came to food, she considered herself quite open-minded and adventurous. At one point, having heard of pizza and there being no pizzeria in Juneau, my mother bought a frozen pizza. We heated it in the oven but all agreed that it tasted genuinely terrible. That was it for my mother. She tried it, she didn't like it, and for the rest of her years, she would never try another piece.

Every fall, when we were older, my father flew to Yakutat, a very small coastal town some three hundred miles north of Juneau, to go moose-hunting with his buddies and later with my brother. We particularly liked moose for its resemblance to beef and its lack of "gaminess," unlike venison. Two moose (the limit), and we were good for a year of meat, which we stored, along with fish and venison, in a large, white, console-style freezer in our basement. The moose had to be skinned and cleaned and shipped back to Juneau on a plane. Alan remembers he and my dad butchering it on the ping-pong table in our basement, while I remember our taking it to the cold storage for butchering into all the familiar cuts — moose steak, moose loin, moose roast, moose shank, moose ribs, mooseburger, moose stew, and moose bones for the dog.

One year, my father put his two moose on the plane but remained in Yakutat for work. We went to the airport to meet the plane, but Juneau was socked in. The airport rests on the tidal flats in a bowl between large mountains looming on three sides, making for one of the world's more perilous landings. Passengers can see tree tops go by as the plane clears the hill, headed for the runway. We waited in suspense to see if the fog would lift so the southbound plane could land, but no such luck. Instead, after hours of circling, it finally over-headed south to Ketchikan. The next day, we again dutifully went to the airport, this time to meet the northbound plane coming from Ketchikan, but Juneau was still socked in, so it circled and over-headed north, back to Anchorage. Juneau remained socked in for five days, and for five days all planes, going both directions, over-headed. By the time the weather finally cleared, we and the airline had lost all trace of the two moose--no small affair since each weighed well over a thousand pounds. Many days and many long-distance calls later, just when we were ready to give up, we got a call from the Ketchikan cold storage company, where someone had kindly pulled the two moose off the plane and stored them. So, once more, we trekked to the airport, this time to successfully meet our missing moose. God bless Alaskans, who know adversity and really do take care of each other!

The kicker, however, was that the Alaska State Legislature was scheduled to meet that very week in

Juneau. Legislators, coming from all over Alaska, were on the original plane and spent five days following the exact same itinerary as our wandering moose (except for the cold storage part). This reignited the fierce and long-running controversy over whether the Alaska State Capitol should be moved to a more accessible location, say, in Anchorage. Juneau immediately invested in a new State office building, jettisoning the subject for another decade.

Home Life

My mother was concerned that, growing up in this remote frontier setting, we would lack the social skills needed to feel comfortable in a larger world. So, she set about civilizing us. The table had to be set properly, fork on the left, napkin (which we never used) folded and placed under it, with the loose corner to the bottom closest to the plate for ease of unfurling; knife and spoon on the right; glass in the nook formed by the knife and spoon, skills she no doubt learned while majoring in Home Economics.

Mom loved to dance and believed it was an essential social skill. So, she gathered up Louise Howerter and Nancy Reddekopp, my friends who lived nearest, and gave us dance lessons on Saturday mornings. We did some childish versions of the waltz, the foxtrot, tap, and a variety of ballroom dances. Her efforts were miserably lost on me. Self-conscious, lacking rhythm, unable to untangle my feet, I simply wished that I could be playing in the creek or hiking through the woods. I was your quintessential tomboy, with my childish aspiration having now morphed from the cowboy in New Mexico to the mountain man of the Daniel Boone legends. Her training efforts ran their course soon enough. I'm still not a dancer and have had the good fortune to marry a man of similar disposition. Unfortunately, I'm completely lost when it comes to music, art, and culture. But I do know how to set a table.

"Mommy, I'm bored." "Mommy, what can I do?" Summer days were long, particularly with both parents at work. Playmates lived far away and there was no TV for us yet. My mother was quite creative, however. She got me a lesson book and a harmonica, and I learned to play, repeating my favorite, "Red River Valley," until all around me cried for mercy. She was great with crafts. I wove reed baskets, pounded nail-hole designs into dismantled tin cans, and did wood-burning. I assembled puzzles and dutifully finished paint-by-number sets. I embroidered from the time I was five. Later I learned to crochet, knit, and sew. And even later I carved boxes, bowls, and totems, using the Tlingit clan motifs, which I love. I enjoy using my hands.

My mother had acquired a vintage Underwood upright typewriter so, when I was nine, she bought a typing manual. "Here," she handed it to me. "Learn to type." I found myself intrigued by typing and, over a matter of weeks, became proficient. Now what? My mother, with whom I often cooked and baked, suggested that I type her recipes for my favorite dishes onto 3"x 5" cards, which I stored in a small, green metal box. "You will want these when you get married and have a family," she suggested, a circumstance quite beyond my imagination, but it made a good project. To this day I still have the little green box of recipes. And when I finished my recipes, I set about typing hers, which were handwritten, for her. At the age of 10, it took only one attempt at typing my homework to teach me that by doing so I stood only to embarrass myself with both teachers and classmates. So, typing was of limited use in the short run, but it was my best skill ever in the long run.

I appreciated the fact that my parents played with us. In the evenings, our favorite pastime was playing cards. Our two staples were Pitch and Rummy, but we also played dominoes, Sorry!, Pollyanna, Parcheesi, or other board games. I never learned to play poker, a game enjoyed by all the rest of my family. My mother also taught us Solitaire, which we played incessantly to pass the time and to which, now in its electronic forms, I am still nearly addicted.

In those days, the radio provided the entertainment now offered by TV. Our imaginations supplied the visual images. After school, I faithfully listened to the *Lone Ranger* on Mondays and Wednesdays, the *Cisco Kid* on Tuesdays and Thursdays, and *Gene Autry* on Fridays, all while eating peanut butter and crackers and setting the table. In the evenings, it was *Our Miss Brooks*, *The FBI in Peace and War*, *Suspense*, *Inner Sanctum*, *The Creaking Door*, *Dragnet*, *Gunsmoke*, and *Jack Benny*. My father liked *Amos n' Andy*, *Fibber McGee and Molly*, and, on Sunday afternoons, he could occasionally be found listening to *Texaco's Symphony Hall* as he puttered around in his basement workshop. My mother teased him, calling it "Sympathy Hall."

Uncomfortable with emotion, my father expressed his love through action, especially by doing things for us. In the run-up to my eighth birthday, I was firmly instructed not to enter the garage — which, of course, I promptly did. And there, under construction, to my eyes, sat the most exquisitely beautiful, child-sized bedroom vanity that I could ever imagine. I was moved to tears. He made me a pair of stilts. He not only put an inflatable army surplus raft in the deep eddy of our creek in which we could play, but erected an army-surplus tent between our old house and the garage for my brother and me to use as a clubhouse. There I spent endless hours lounging on an army-surplus cot, drinking Kool-Aid, and reading and re-reading library books (heavy on Nancy Drew, the Bobbsey Twins, and the Hardy Boys) and comic books (especially Mickey Mouse, Donald Duck, Archie, and the Lone Ranger). And when we got older, he erected a ping-pong table in our basement, starting first with a piece of plywood and two sawhorses and progressing to construction of a regulation-size table. Following a long absence when I was a teenager, he brought me a gift — a very expensive perfume — which I have kept to this day.

As a young child, I was deeply hurt by his unbridled enthusiasm for and favoritism toward my brother, knowing that there was nothing I could do to change the fact that I had been born a girl. But mitigating this circumstance was the fact that, during these years, my brother was too young to do many things with my father, and so he turned to me. I interpreted his wanting my company as an expression of love. Thus, I felt honored and loved when he invited me to join him on a trip to the gravel pit, the garbage dump, the hardware store or the lumberyard, or to do an errand on our boat. In later years, it was an invitation to go duck hunting and in high school, it was an invitation to spend the weekend with him in Sitka, where he had been stationed for one of his survey assignments. Wanting to "be with" was an important expression of love in my family.

When I was nine, I got a junior-sized bicycle for my birthday and my mother, bless her heart, taught me to ride, running endlessly behind me on the road while trying to protect me from disaster. It seemed like I was forever destined to crash into ditches, trees, bridge posts, or, when lacking any other alternative, just to wipe out on the plain gravel road. We must have gone through a truckload of band-aids before I finally learned the arts of staying upright, steering, and braking. As much as I loved my tricycle when I was small, I loved my bicycle even more. It was blue, my favorite color, a steel American bike with balloon tires, foot brakes, and no gears, purchased from Sears Roebuck. Their J.C. Higgins brand was not as prestigious, nor as expensive, as my friends' Schwinns. Unknowingly, we installed its handlebars backwards, giving the bike its own peculiar look and cramping the space available for my knees. Nevertheless, it was pure liberty — the ability to go beyond the circle of walkability and not have to ask for a ride. When I grew older it was replaced with a full-sized bike (handle bars pointed in the right direction this time) and one of my favorite activities was packing a picnic lunch and going biking with my friends, around the Loop Road, to Mendenhall Glacier and the Skater's Cabin, up the remote road to Montana Creek, to the airport, "out the road" to tiny clusters of homes known as Tee Harbor and occasionally even into Juneau. And if friends weren't available, I was happy to go exploring on my own.

Auke Bay in 1953 was a very small, isolated community. Everyone knew everyone else and their business and the only strangers who came through, other than tourists, were Jehovah's Witnesses and salesmen of various varieties: Fuller brushes, encyclopedias, vacuum cleaners or Bibles. All were *persona non grata* to our family. One day that summer an unfamiliar car pulled up to the end of our long driveway; a portly, balding,

Ronda and Alan, summer in Auke Bay.

middle-aged man in a suit got out and walked up to where we were weeding the garden. He was selling the *Encyclopedia Britannica*. My mother barely looked at him, told him flatly that she wasn't interested, and kept right on weeding. He probably sensed that he had spotted a hard-working, upwardly mobile family whose only goals in life were to provide economic security and opportunity to their children — exactly the market he was looking for. He began his pitch. How essential encyclopedias were to our education. How they would lead to our success in life. What a good investment they were. How they could be financed with a great credit plan. What an important message we would be receiving from our parents.

My mother wasn't buying it. She reiterated that she wasn't interested. He just couldn't believe he couldn't make this sale. She continued weeding. As he struggled for the winning argument, he began toeing the cabbages my mother had just weeded. Already angry, she was growing more and more so. Then came the trigger. "If your children turn out to be ignorant, it will be your fault," he declared, challenging her entire life purpose. With this, my mother silently laid down her hoe. Uttering not a word, she walked into the house only to re-emerge moments later on the top step of our stoop with a shotgun in her hand. She took direct aim at him. The man took off at a run down our long driveway. Who would guess that a portly, middle-aged gentleman in a suit could move so fast? My brother and I, who had soberly observed the whole episode, were speechless. We just looked at each other wide-eyed and then dissolved into laughter.

School

When I arrived in Juneau in 1950, at the age of seven, Auke Bay had no schools. We were bussed fifteen miles to Juneau, which had a high-school — Capitol School — and a grade school — Fifth Street School — both built identically side-by-side on the steep hill overlooking downtown Juneau. We had a gym but no cafeteria. Many town children went home for lunch while those of us living "out-the-road" brought ours — mine invariably peanut butter and jelly, tuna fish, or bologna with mayonnaise on white bread, an orange or apple, and a thermos of milk, in a metal lunchbox of which there were two versions: brick shaped gray with plain red or blue sides or barn-shaped, usually solid black or silver, both imbued with a unique lunchbox smell.

Schools in Juneau were impressive. They were nearly a full year ahead of the Woods Gormley School in Santa Fe, but I quickly caught up with the assistance of my second-grade teacher, Mrs. Druxman. Schools were community-oriented, taking responsibility for such things as vaccinations. During the height of the polio scare, the school system assured that every child received gamma globulin as a preventive measure.

(Credit: Alaska State Library Historical Collection)

Fifth Street School and Capitol School. Elementary (left) High School (right).

While the Fifth Street School had a playground, I recollect no playground equipment. I do remember once leaning against the school yard fence and learning indelibly why you never put your lips against metal in sub-zero weather. We entertained ourselves primarily with games of marbles, jump rope, Red Rover, Mother May I?, and 7-Up, a competitive ball game played against a wall. After school, while waiting a half-hour for the school bus, we frequented the Alaska State Museum on the fourth floor of the Federal Building just across the street and below our school. Despite admonitions not to touch the exhibits, the small, stuffed black bear bore all the signs of a beloved a rocking horse.

Our grade was accommodated by four classrooms. By the time I reached third grade, the school had become so overcrowded that the auditorium was jerry-rigged into classrooms and my class got the walled-off stage. The following year Harborview, a beautiful new elementary school down on the flats, opened. In the seventh grade, it was back to the Fifth Street School, and, in eighth grade, the town of Douglas, across Gastineau Channel, consolidated its schools with those of Juneau. All eighth graders were bused to Douglas, adding forty-five minutes to our already hour-and-a-quarter commute. In my freshman year, the new high school opened, located next door to Harborview.

Seldom, if ever, did Juneau have electrical storms and most children had never experienced lightening or thunder. One stormy morning in the third grade, however, the class was bewildered by a sudden flash of light followed by an enormous clap of thunder rolling over Juneau. My classmates instantly "ducked and covered" under their desks, imagining that it could only be the cold war attack for which they had been trained. Overcoming her surprise, Ms. Downs, newly arrived from "the states" where such weather was commonplace, assured us that it was only a thunderstorm and that we were all safe.

In my fifth-grade year, the first jet to Alaska flew over Juneau on its way to Anchorage. The principal rang the fire alarm and we all poured onto the school yard to watch as this tiny, sparkling silver speck make its way slowly, high across the azure sky. My brother, then in kindergarten, ran across the playground watching the plane, and declared that he couldn't see what the big deal was — after all, he could run faster than the plane. No one could convince him otherwise.

That year the first prop-jet made its inaugural flight to Juneau. To celebrate, Pacific Northern Airlines offered several free "trips to nowhere" that day. A

Pacific Northern Airline Constellation (Prop-Jet).

(Credit: Ed Coates Collection)

neighbor, Bud Tickell, got tickets and grabbed his son Bruce, my brother, and me out of school. I was torn, being a very conscientious student and proud of my perfect attendance record. But I was also excited to add the first airplane ride to my list of "firsts" (not counting the Piper Cub experience when I was three). My teacher did not share our excitement, however, and in disapproval, docked me a half-day's absence and a half grade on my report card for missing a quiz. This was a small penalty for a momentous occasion.

In the sixth grade, we were offered band and chorus. I chose band, and, under the influence of my mother, I decided to play the saxophone. Her logic was, "Play an unusual instrument and you'll get more opportunities." In a conversation with friends in adulthood, we all laughed to find that our mothers had all given us precisely the same counsel. Among us were oboe, French horn, saxophone, piccolo and a tuba player. Not a single trumpet or clarinet. Not even a flute. I have no background and little talent in music, but my mother was right.

My "unusual" choice of the saxophone allowed me to play in the pep band at basketball games (then Juneau's only major sport, given the weather) and later to attend the Alaska Music Festival which brought together competing high school bands from

Southeastern Alaska — Haines, Skagway, Juneau, Sitka, Wrangell, Petersburg, and Ketchikan — rotated among different towns every two years. During my tenure, our band travelled to Sitka where we stayed and performed at Mt. Edgecombe, a residential school for native Alaskans run by the Bureau of Indian Affairs. Travelling to another town, much less being allowed to explore it independently, was a big deal. Listening to a festival recording years later, I can't believe how bad we sounded.

Art was taught by Max Lewis and here I was more talented. In the manner of art teachers, he did not so much teach as help us explore our own talents and different mediums. A conservation group in Juneau sponsored an annual poster contest and, with his encouragement, I won first prize and received a $50 bond one year for a poster showing a silhouetted stag framed by crosshairs against a beautiful sunset. Forty years later, I found the bond, still uncashed, in a box of papers.

School Bus Tales
We were at the beginning of the school bus route and the ride to Juneau was an hour and a quarter each way. This meant leaving at 7:15 a.m. and returning at 4:45 p.m., in the dark both times during the winter months. I always sat in the second seat behind the driver, by the window,

leaving room for my good friend, Louise Howerter, who got on two stops later, to sit beside me. Deep friendships were sealed by the lengthy times we spent on the bus together. The bus went around the Loop Road which encircled Glacier Valley — the long way to town. Our bus driver, Bill Spaulding, was a fisherman during the summer. He was a short, stocky, gruff man known to speak only in monosyllables or — better yet — to grunt. He had little interest in or patience with children. To emphasize the point, he prominently displayed a razor strap in the front of the bus, as a warning to us all.

We were expected to be on the shoulder of the road when the bus pulled up. If we weren't, the bus would wait three minutes. If there were signs that we were on our way, it would continue to wait. If not, it would leave. The Hurlock's, living on the back side of Loop Road, were notorious. A Catholic family with six boys, their house was set back easily a quarter mile from the road. The first — usually the oldest — would come running out of the front door within the requisite three-minute limit. Only when he at last reached the bus, did the second appear in the doorway. Collecting all six easily took fifteen minutes. And if any of us missed the bus, that was it. You missed the day. There was no other way to get to school. That experience provided me a handy template for a lifetime of anxiety dreams — the school bus is there waiting, about to pull away. I can't decide what to wear. I can't find my clothes. I can't put them on right. They don't fit. They don't match. They're inappropriate. I can't find my lunch, my jacket, my books. The unimaginable is about to happen. All because I can't get it together.

The school bus experience was largely boredom and bus exhaust, but two colorful incidents, which occurred when I was older, punctuate my memories. In high school, I had a good friend, Doug Dobyns, who boarded the bus on the back side of Loop Road. He was a snare drummer in the school band and while quiet, he had a streak of mischief. Doug always carried his drumsticks in his back pocket, ready to drum on any handy surface. In the winter, vehicles all used chains on the back tires to get through the snow and ice. A sign of trouble was the regular "ping, ping, ping" of the broken chain hitting the vehicle body.

One afternoon we were riding home through a big snowstorm. The snow banks on the side of the road were easily six feet high and the visibility nearly zero. Suddenly, we heard the "ping, ping, ping" of a broken chain. Bill donned his parka, got out and laid down in the snow under the bus to examine the back tires. Nothing amiss. So, he got back in and started the bus. Shortly, again, came the "ping, ping, ping".

He stopped, again donned his parka, got out and once more laid down in the snow to examine the chains. Again, nothing amiss. By now most of us were working hard to keep a straight face. At the third "ping, ping, ping," someone must have giggled, because it suddenly dawned on Bill. The "ping, ping, ping" was not a broken chain at all, but Doug imitating one with his drumsticks on the back of a seat. Spaulding was livid. We had never seen him use the razor strap and we were terrified for Doug. Spaulding stomped, red-faced, to the back of the bus, man-handled Doug down the aisle and bodily thrust him, from the top step of the bus, headlong, into the snow bank. He then grunted, sat back down in the driver's seat and drove away without saying a word. Doug walked home in the snow and the dark that night.

My second school bus memory is of one spring afternoon when we had major rain storms and ice jammed the rivers and creeks. With about ten of us still left to deliver, our bus reached Montana Creek, one the most remote and deserted parts of the Loop Road, only to find the creek had overflowed causing a large flood. Bill stopped the bus and then slowly pulled forward into the water. He proceeded further and further as the water rose higher and higher on the bus; our eyes grew wider and wider and we all held our breath. Finally, at about two-and-a-half feet, the water reached the engine, which promptly sputtered and died. After unsuccessfully trying to restart the engine and stewing around for a while, Bill exited the back door into waist-deep water, to go for help — no small affair with no traffic on the road, no houses or people nearby, and no phones even if there had been.

Time passed slowly, and it grew dark as we sat in the stalled bus. Never in anyone's recollection had a school bus not appeared on its appointed rounds. The older kids comforted the little ones who became frightened and began to fall apart. Finally, a couple of hours later, a tow truck and a second school bus appeared behind us. The tow truck reached our bus, pulled it back onto dry land, we were able to exit, board the second bus and go home the long way, circling back around the Loop to get to Auke Bay. We got home about 7:00 p.m. that night. The incident evoked withering remarks about Bill's IQ for months to come among families and parents in Auke Bay.

One thing the Juneau area did quite well, however, was plough snow. In my eleven years of school there, we only ever had a single snow day and it occurred the morning after a storm that left well over four feet of snow. Despite a three-foot stoop, we couldn't even open our front door. Eager for a challenge and always game for a heroic effort, I set forth to shovel our long driveway by myself. I started out shoveling the width of the driveway. The further I got, however, the narrower grew my shoveled path. My parents were impressed and appreciative, even if my father had to go out and trim it up.

The Wilderness

The environs of Auke Bay and Southeastern Alaska are part of a vast wilderness known as the Tongass National Forest. A few steps off the beaten path took you to places previously untouched by humans. The wilderness is a rain forest, with the ground made virtually impassable by centuries of fallen, crisscrossed, moss-covered, and decaying trees, layered helter-skelter atop each other with muskeg (mossy swamp) of indeterminant depth underneath, all overgrown by dense ground cover including moss, ferns, berry bushes, skunk cabbage and thorny devil's club.

We shared the wilderness with abundant wildlife. Beavers inhabited Auke Lake, a freshwater lake a couple of miles in diameter and a mile from the bay, building a lodge on the unsettled and inaccessible far side of the lake. One year, the lake began to rise mysteriously, although there had been no unusual rainfall. Finally, the men of the community organized a work party to search for the cause, only to find that the

The Wilderness.

beavers had built a dam across the lake's outlet. They dynamited the dam; the water level fell and man and beaver somehow managed to live peaceably together thereafter. I later learned that beavers do this because they are very mobile in the water and almost totally immobile on land. When they've eaten all the foliage accessible to the shoreline, they build or heighten a dam, raise the water level, and go back for a second helping. Not dumb, they. This often explains dead trees seen protruding from a lake.

Nature, while stunning, is utterly indifferent to and unforgiving of humans. Everyone knew someone who drowned in a fishing accident, was killed in a plane crash, died in a fire, encountered a bear, or got lost in the wilderness, never to return. The wilderness surrounded and engulfed everything, coming to within yards of our houses and roads. Growing up, the chief guarantor of our safety was fear, carefully and systematically instilled in us by our parents, mostly my mother. It was only as an adult, revisiting Auke Bay, that I realized how pervasive and constricting was the fear that we had been taught.

We ventured only yards into the woods, never losing sight of civilization, unless it was on a charted trail. Only two of the countless mountains surrounding the area had trails. The others, as far as we knew, had never been climbed. The black waters of Auke Lake dropped off precipitously at the shore line. A myth prevailed that it was bottomless and had an undertow, so no one dreamt of swimming in it. Mendenhall River, swiftly flowing from the lake in front of the glacier through Glacier Valley to the sea, was so laden with cement-gray silt as to be opaque. You couldn't see your hand three inches below the surface. If we fell in, we were told, the silt would weigh down our clothes and drag us to the bottom.

The bears of Auke Bay replaced the snakes of New Mexico as my chief talisman of fear. Auke Bay hosted two kinds of bear. Most prominent were the black bears, which are smaller and generally uninterested in encounters with humans, unless that encounter puts you between a mother bear and her cubs. Rarer, and far larger, more aggressive, and unpredictable, are brown bears. When we walked in the woods, we were instructed to carry no unsealed food, to make noise — whistle, sing, talk, anything — and to be alert, keeping our eyes and ears open. If we confronted a bear we were to freeze, not look it in the eye, and slowly, ever so slowly, back away. Then, get the hell out of there. The black bears loved Lake Creek during the salmon run. While instilling us with the fear of bears, my father, capable of his own small mischief, would sneak into the backyard and lay bacon strips on a tree stump, luring the bear in order to see it up close — that is until the day my mother caught him.

No one we knew shot bears because no one ate their meat. They are also not easy to take down and a wounded bear is wild, unpredictable, and a danger to all. Every year or two, a "Cheechako" (newcomer), in some flight of machismo or romanticism, would shoot, but fail to kill a bear. Then, to protect the community, the men would organize a hunting party, search until they found the bear and finish the job. I remember many rants by my father on this subject.

Later, when we were in high school, Doug Dobyns and another good friend, Lee Hagmeier, went fishing up on Montana Creek, a particularly remote and isolated area. In heavy underbrush, they walked into a brown bear which, surprised, delivered Lee a swat that destroyed his face, threatened his life and blinded him forever.

We were taught, if ever lost, to follow a stream downhill. This lesson served Doug Dobyns and me well when, in high school, we scaled the nearest and relatively low mountain across Glacier Valley which had no trail. Upon arriving at the summit, we found fog swirling in around us as we ate our lunch. We started down, only mildly concerned that we did not see the precise landmarks of our earlier climb. It didn't take long for us to realize that we were lost and to find a creek and follow it down. A hard way to go, but it did the trick. We had accidently come down the back side of the mountain (easy to do if you make a slight miscalculation at the summit). We arrived at the bottom many hours later, in the dark, emerging at the Switzer Creek Bridge, cold, soaked, and muddy, miles from our point of departure; we hitch-hiked home. I didn't even know that the mountain behind Switzer Creek was the same mountain I saw from our front window every day. And I never told my mother.

Unnamed and untamed, this mountain has a special place in my heart. At once it was so common yet so magnificent, sharing its many moods each day from our front windows. It was later dubbed "Thunder Mountain," probably by real estate agents and only recently, following an attempt to name it after a

Thunder Mountain.

prominent Juneauite, did I discover that it had long been named by the Tlingit people — Tleixsatanjin meaning "Idle Hands at Rest." It now has a trail and its west end has been made partially accessible to all-terrain vehicles. Rarely am I disturbed by progress, since the wilderness is so vast, but I can't help feeling a bit wistful that this great, silent, pristine giant, so close and yet so far, so familiar yet so remote, has been diminished and the very intimate and awesome experience with which we were blessed will not be available to others.

Chapter THREE

Living on Auke Lake: 1953 to 1964

Almost immediately upon moving into our Lake Creek house, my parents decided that it was too small, too poorly-built, and too old for their liking, so they began to seek another property on which to build. They found five acres on the same road, a quarter mile closer to Auke Bay — on a hill which looked out over Auke Lake. From the hill was a magnificent view of the lake and Thunder Mountain on the far side of Glacier Valley. The US government was then encouraging development, and so we homesteaded, an arrangement by which, in return for five thousand dollars in improvements over a five-year period, the government would cede the land for a dollar. My father surveyed the land and designed the house; we cut and cleared the trees, and first brought in a caterpillar to excavate for the driveway, yard, and house. The "cat"

was rendered useless, however, by the intractable gray clay that lay beneath a thin layer of topsoil, forcing us to next bring in a steam shovel, which finally did the job. To build a house today, you would ordinarily hire a contractor, but in Auke Bay in the 1950s, no such concept existed. You did it yourself. So again, by day my parents earned a living and by nights and on weekends built the house.

Since, at age eight, I was of little help in construction, my job was to entertain myself and my three-year-old brother. My chief memory is of utter and total boredom, but two house-building stories stand out. My older cousin, Albert, age fifteen, came to visit us from New Mexico the summer we started the house and the first story is his. He worked alongside my father and, on this particular weekend, the task was to remove stumps after

Cousin Albert, myself and Alan.

the trees had been cleared. To break up and dislodge the stumps, my father had carefully packed blasting caps in the back of a borrowed pick-up truck. As he and Albert worked throughout the day, he endlessly cautioned Albert on the danger of blasting caps and how carefully they must be handled. Late in the afternoon, when they were tired and ready to leave, a neighbor dropped by. My father could lose himself in a conversation and so, as this conversation came to an end, my father absent-mindedly bent over and tossed his tools and materials into the back of the truck, landing on top of the remaining blasting caps. Albert reports ducking. Miraculously, Armageddon did not occur that afternoon. Albert and my dad did not die, although I'm sure that Albert lost several years of longevity. He did not tell me this story until decades later. I'm perfectly certain that my mother never knew.

While the culture of Alaska emphasized individualism and self-sufficiency, the harshness of the environment also fed a culture of community and collective responsibility. None of these values was explicit; I don't know how exactly they were communicated, but the message was nevertheless strong and clear. Everyone turned out when a family was in need, or there was a community project — be it building the church or the American Legion hall. All able-bodied men belonged to the volunteer fire department. If someone owned a snowplow, they helped plow the driveways of elderly neighbors. If someone was walking, you gave them a ride. If one woman was making a shopping trip into Juneau, she invited other women in the neighborhood to join.

Our new house on Auke Lake.

It was understood that our neighbor, Hal Weidner, with an electrical background, would do the wiring. Other neighbors would offer help or their special expertise. No one had to ask. Mutual help was understood. Simply getting the word out was sufficient. The Saturday morning my parents began pouring the basement of our new house, some twenty men from the community turned up to work for the day, shoveling sand and cement, mixing it, hauling it and pouring it into rebar-reinforced forms. The work was back-breaking and couldn't stop until the job was complete. The crew worked into the evening. One window in the back wall was set ever so slightly crooked, allegedly because Stanley Reddikopp, then a teenager and son of our neighbor, Ellwood, was in a hurry to go on a date that evening. While my father, the perfectionist, rued this as a flaw, I looked at it as a symbol of a community in which, young or old, we all came together in support, whenever it was ever needed.

Auke Lake

The sweeping expanse of Auke Lake, now a few hundred yards from our house, provided an endless source of fascination and recreation, although never swimming. The lake was large, surrounded with steep, wooded hills and underbrush that fell dramatically down to a shoreline garnished by fallen logs and lily pads. From our front windows we could watch its many moods and the changing flora and fauna, including the beavers, bear, ducks, geese, eagles, and other wildlife it nurtured. We could see the salmon jump, announcing their arrival in late August and bringing with them the rainbow trout that feasted on their eggs. A few houses on the lake shared our view but most notably, the Chapel-by-the-Lake, a community-built log chapel located a couple of miles around the lakeshore, looked out from a hill on a world-famous view of the lake, Mendenhall Glacier and the mountains surrounding it.

The bears loved Auke Lake as well. One had a daily routine so regular that we could set our clock by his travels. During the summer, it would appear around 4:00 p.m. at a distant point on the lake, then disappear into the underbrush. Ten minutes later, it would re-emerge, trundle across the road and again disappear into the underbrush. Another ten minutes later and it would lumber up the hill, right past the oil tank beside our house and up into the woods.

On clear nights in the wintertime, the expanse of the lake offered front row seats to the aurora borealis — huge, breath-taking, multicolored curtains of light sweeping back and forth across the night sky, capable of instilling awe and religion in the most hard-hearted of non-believers.

Shortly after moving to our new house, my father put a ten-foot wooden rowboat on the lake, so we could go rowing whenever we wished. The rowboat provided enormous solace for the turbulent years of my adolescence, a place I could go to be alone, sulk, read, meditate, create fantasies, and feel the awe of nature. By myself, I explored the otherwise unreachable far shores of the lake and many times I would simply lay down the oars, stretch out on a seat and lose myself in the clouds of the summer sky as the boat swayed gently in the wind.

In the winter, the lake froze over. After several days of cold weather, Dad would drill a hole to test the depth of the ice and would allow us out on it accordingly. On cold nights, as the ice thickened and expanded, it would crack producing booms that were just short of sonic. The frozen lake became a social magnet, drawing

View of Auke Lake from our front windows.

all those who otherwise lived so distant from each other together onto the lake. After school, we hurried through our homework and dinner so that

Mom and Alan on Auke Lake.

we could skate for a couple of hours before bedtime. By then it was dark, but the moon, the lights of distant houses across the lake and often northern lights, showed the way while the darkness bathed the lake in a lonely, intimate magic. My parents were eager to have us learn and enable us to skate, but they rarely joined in themselves, exhausted by work.

Neighbors gathered in spontaneous skating parties. We played "crack-the-whip" by forming a long line of skaters holding hands. With the line skating quickly in unison, the leader would turn abruptly whipping those down the line with centrifugal force that spun skaters off at high speeds. Daredevils brought their cars out onto the ice, although I never thought this a good idea. Invariably, someone would build a bonfire on the shore and hot dogs and marshmallows would appear. In a funny incident one Sunday afternoon, our church group sponsored a skating party on the lake in front of the Chapel. Toward the end, Ken Smith, the minister, shouted for members to come into the church for hot dogs and ice cream, failing to specify that he meant youth group members; all of the skaters within hearing range immediately poured into the church, necessitating an emergency run to the general store in order not to disappoint.

The Community Driver's Test

My mother was always expecting a disaster for which she diligently prepared us. When I was nine, she insisted that I begin learning to drive. "You never know when something will happen to dad and me, and you'll have to go get help fast," she would declare. In our minds was a recent example. In clearing the land behind our Lake Creek house, she and my Dad attempted a controlled burn. The ground, however, was uncharacteristically dry, and the fire leapt out of control, spread rapidly throughout the clearing and threatened our house. With no hose connections, she and my father beat the fire with wet rags as I ran back and forth to the house to carry water. Neighbors driving by immediately stopped and ran to help and, eventually, we got the fire under control, but the event left a deep impression.

I hated learning to drive. I hated the high stakes of feeling out of control with such a powerful force at my command. I hated sitting on my mom or dad's lap. I hated the mistakes that accompany learning. But I mostly hated the fact that other kids weren't doing it. Heaven forbid, they might see me. I was sure they would tease me forever more. I don't think this happened, but the expectation alone sufficed. This is when I came to appreciate those long, deserted stretches of the Loop Road. By the time I got my learner's permit, it was okay. Other kids were learning to drive as well. My driver's test, however, was an unforgettable event for me and virtually the whole community. And for the first time, I wasn't embarrassed. It was so ludicrous that I could only laugh.

We arranged it on a Thursday, the day my mother and various neighbors piled into our station wagon to go shopping and run errands in Juneau. We stopped first at the supermarket, where everyone loaded up the car with their two-week supply of groceries. Everyone else then went shopping while I went for my driver's test. I was joined in the front seat of our red Chevrolet station wagon by a very nice, young policeman, clearly new to the force. I'm not sure he was even old enough to shave. I had studied the drivers' manual and aced the written test. For the road test, each maneuver was given a penalty value and, if the you accumulated twenty or more points, you failed. At first, the young policeman and I did all right. We drove through the heart of downtown and I missed only one hand signal (this was before the age of built-in turn-signals).

The policeman warned me that, at some point, he would tell me to "stop." When he did, I was to stop as quickly as I could. We were driving down Willoughby at about twenty miles per hour when he shouted "Stop!" and I slammed on the brakes as hard as I could. We screeched to a halt in the middle of the street and the back seat — the bulwark holding back that two-week supply of community groceries — collapsed. Bottles of ketchup, mustard, mayonnaise, household cleaners, cans of vegetables, packages of meat, loaves of bread and cartons of eggs — everything came hurtling into the front seat, crashing down around our heads, shoulders, and feet. I pulled over to the curb, and he and I began picking up groceries. As we worked a large dog, fascinated by our predicament, leaned his front paws up against the window to watch. Both a bit rattled, we finished the job and then proceeded.

Next came the parallel parking test. Three futile tries later, on a virtually empty lot, I found the young policeman giving me instructions and, between the two of us, somehow the car got itself parked. Next, we headed for West Ninth Street, one of the steepest streets in mountainous Juneau, where he told me I would have to stop, put on the emergency brake, turn off the engine, and then restart the car and proceed up the hill. On cue, at the steepest point and in the middle of a sharp curve, I stopped. He looked at me quizzically and I inquired what was wrong. "I thought at least you might pull over," he said. "You didn't tell me that," I replied with the literalness of a child. Cars began to jam up ahead and behind us, their drivers unhappy at being subjected to the same driver's test that I was. There were no automatic transmissions in those days. Somehow I managed to simultaneously shift into first gear, ease up on the clutch, press the gas pedal and release the emergency brake so I wouldn't plow backwards into the cars lining up behind me.

Finally, the test was over, and we pulled up to the police station. He completed the scorecard, threw it at me and literally fled the car. I looked at it. The score was a very generous nineteen penalty points. I'm sure he knew that, if he flunked me, I would simply return the very next week, and he would face the same traumatic experience all over again — a thought he clearly didn't relish. To myself, I vowed to forever maintain my license such that never again would I ever have to do another road test. And I've pretty well succeeded. Once they sorted out their groceries, my driver's test provided a source of hilarity for those families and ours, for years to come.

A Baby Sister Is Born (1956)

Shortly after my thirteenth birthday, my little sister, Lynn, was born. We were all excited. Her advent became my avocation. I relished the tiny clothes and baby equipment which our neighbors bestowed on us, refinished the used crib we were given (I now hate to think what was in the paint I used), and knitted her a

My sister, Lynn, as a newborn.

light yellow and green checkered sweater. Both I and my friends were thrilled that October, in the eighth grade, when my father came to school to give me the news and to take me to meet her for the first time. Considerable family consultation resulted in her being named Lynnette Jean. Every day I looked forward to coming home to this new little person, who immediately grew into an endless source of joy and entertainment. I was eager to help, which my mother always appreciated, but she made it clear that she would not place the responsibility for raising Lynn on me. My role would always be voluntary. Above all else she was fair and reasonable.

My mother and Lynn, age eight months.

When Lynn was slightly over a year old, she brought unwanted drama into our lives. I was at choir practice one night when the organist, a neighbor who was also a nurse, nearly missed practice. We knew something was seriously wrong. When she finally arrived, she warned me to sit down. She had just come from our house, where Lynn had stopped breathing, turned blue and passed out. My mother, ever prepared for disaster, administered CPR and by the time our neighbor arrived, Lynn had been revived. I nearly passed out myself. My heart filled with terror, my eyes filled with tears, and my head tried to process this potentially catastrophic, life-changing event that almost happened but didn't quite.

Apparently, after letting out a big cry, which babies regularly do, an anomaly in Lynn's throat caused her to be unable to catch her breath. We had no idea what would happen if she were alone when this happened with no one there to revive her. We surely didn't care to find out. It happened several more times until she reached the age at which she outgrew such crying. During those years, we tiptoed as if on eggshells, fearing that each cry might be her last and that something we did or didn't do would be the cause. The experience, occurring so young, no doubt bent the arc of her early development and in part caused my mother to become extremely protective of her. She was only four when I went away to college. I adored her, missed her terribly and sadly ended up missing most of her childhood.

School Stories

In the seventh grade, for the first time, teachers specialized and rotated between classes. Mrs. Green taught grammar and literature. A remarkably skilled teacher, she taught me all the grammar I ever needed to know in a single semester. Mr. Kumitat, a young new teacher, taught math and science. He was a cold, volatile, and occasionally cruel man, never hesitating to humiliate students. One day, in a pop quiz of five questions, he had one answer wrong, giving everyone in the class a score of 80% or worse. Student after student approached his desk to challenge him, which only resulted in escalating nastiness and intransigency on his part. I watched as he angrily sent student after student away, eventually yelling at them and even disparaging them. "Why on earth would you repeat a tactic that was so obviously failing?" I wondered to myself. So finally, when the dust settled, in my most respectful manner, I approached his desk to tell him I simply did not know how to do the problem. I asked if he would please walk me through it, whereupon he stumbled upon his error. My plan worked. Innately I knew that frontal encounters don't work, especially when you have no power. And putting people on the defensive never works.

Math was taught dreadfully in grade school. From my experience, you could have believed that math was a rote and mechanical endeavor. So, elementary algebra in high school presented the first real challenge. It was taught by Michael Kirk, a small, wiry man with a heavy German accent and a Germanically-complicated mind. Whenever I asked for help in understanding the solution to a problem, he answered by showing yet a different solution, now giving me two solutions I didn't understand. If I asked again, he added a third to my growing bouquet of incomprehensible solutions. Clearly, we were out of the realm of the rote and mechanical — the point at which many women get aced out of math — and I couldn't think in mathematical terms. Nevertheless, I felt the pressure to get a good grade. He required a term paper and I chose a topic that had to do with measuring the distance to stars, leaning heavily on encyclopedias and the assistance of my father, the engineer. I submitted the paper, which Mr. Kirk thought was brilliant, and that bought me an "A" for the course. Decades later, at a reunion, I was surprised to find that he remembered not only me but also the paper, which he had kept with him all these years.

Our basketball coach taught chemistry. Mr. Eide was a tall, gawky, balding, easy-going man with a large Adam's apple, who reminded me of a crane. He didn't seem to take anything too seriously. He walked around the chemistry lab evoking Rube Goldberg to describe our experiments and sarcastically muttering the mantra that, "If a little will do a little good, then a lot more will do a lot more." He loved practical jokes and occasionally would pour a heavy, invisible gas on the floor which produced loud "pops" as we walked into it.

Mr. Eide would hand out exams and disappear to the teacher's lounge for the hour, whereupon cheating was rampant. I was indignant and vented to my mother. Without consulting me, she went directly to the principal, and Mr. Eide was furious. I'm not sure he ever knew that I was the source. It took only this one lesson for me to learn to be very careful what you tell your mother. I did fine in the first semester, which was inorganic chemistry (very rote and mechanical) but hung on by my fingernails for the second, when we studied organic chemistry. To make the grade, I took on every available extra credit project. One was the etching of glass with hydrogen fluoride. Calling on my artistic skills, I etched lovely designs onto several paraffin-covered kitchen glasses. Mr. Eide was so pleased that for several weeks he proudly displayed my glasses as he walked through the halls and to the teachers' lounge. I got an "A" in the class. Damned! Like algebra, I was highly aware that I had cut corners and failed to learn the basics but, if those are their rules, it's not my fault for using them to my advantage.

Social Life (Or Lack Thereof)

Did I say that living in Auke Bay was isolating for a child? Early on I formed three or four close friendships with girls whose homes were within walking distance, sealed by the long hours we spent together on the school bus. I remained lifelong friends with Louise Howerter and JoAn Lynch (sadly, Louise died in the late 1990s). Living at such a distance precluded playing after school or on weekends with kids who lived in town, curtailing the opportunities to foster their friendships. And while my parents did their best to support my participation in after-school, evening, and weekend social activities, all of these took place in Juneau, and the distance, combined with the weather, inevitably hobbled my participation. I knew transportation was a burden, so in most cases, I self-censored and simply didn't ask.

My two best friends. Louise Howerter (top) and JoAn Lynch.

I wasn't much of a joiner, but because all my girlfriends were doing it, I joined first Brownie Scouts and later the Girl Scouts, which met after school. The high point of Scouts was summer camp at Eagle River. A bus took us about twenty miles to the north, to the end of the road, and then we hiked in for two miles to reach the camp. Baggage and goods were delivered by boat. Camp was ecstasy. The woods, the beach, the crafts, the games, the singing, the campfires, the fellowship, the independence, the outdoor living — all appealed to my tomboy nature. We lived in big, army-surplus house tents furnished with eight cots each and erected on wooden platforms. Bathrooms were outhouses. Both tents and outhouses had to be cleaned each day.

There I learned to swim. The camp had an extremely gentle beach that went out for nearly a half mile before the water grew deep. The instructor had us sit down in a foot-and-a-half of water, spread our arms, and simply lay back. Voila! The body floats (especially in salt water)! I was so enamored that on the second day I decided to see how long I could float. The next thing I knew the kids were yelling from the distant shore and a counselor was swimming furiously to reach me as I floated blissfully out to sea. As for learning to swim, all I needed was the confidence of knowing that my body would float and I could take it from there. The next year, belonging to Girls Scouts became the means to an end, which was summer camp. The anti-authoritarianism in me disliked the requirements for earning badges, and my independence — if not arrogance — led me to think I already knew what the Scout book had to offer.

With encouragement from my mother, I was more serious about 4-H (head, hands, heart and health), which taught practical skills — primarily baking, sewing and gardening. The Club was led by Virginia Walpole, the good-hearted wife of our car mechanic, whose daughter was too young even to participate. We met at her house, not far from Auke Bay, every two weeks. Not only did we participate in the annual 4-H Fair with all its exhibitions and competitions, but we also built a float each year and marched proudly in the Fourth of July parade. 4-H presented me with a conflict of authority. I had already learned many of the skills from my mother who was extremely practical, distained any unnecessary work, and was known for taking short-cuts. I considered the demanding standards of 4-H largely make-work, but I grudgingly complied in order to compete successfully at the annual 4-H Fair. I was a very loyal daughter.

In high school, many of the girls joined Rainbow Girls, a Masonic youth organization and, feeling social pressure, I joined as well. While billed as a service organization, all I remember was that it required the wearing of formals and sponsored dances. I found much of the pseudo-religious masonic ritual to be mumbo-jumbo and, when I discovered within a year or two that membership was not going to address my sense of belonging, I quit.

Family Leisure

It wasn't until the late 1950's when I was in high school that we got a TV. TV transmissions came from Juneau but reception in an area as rugged and remote as Auke Bay was largely theoretical. TV programs must have been shipped on a slow boat from Seattle, because they were always two weeks late. Watching TV led to a family ritual that was a mix of frustration and hilarity, however. Getting reception required three people — one person holding the antenna (which was replaced over time by ever larger versions) and wandering randomly around our large front yard, one person standing on the porch and transmitting feedback and instructions back-and-forth, and one person at the TV, twirling the dials and reporting the outcome. For a transitory moment, the TV image would clear, and the command to stop would be sent down chain to the person holding the antenna, who would then do their best to implant it in that exact spot in our yard. As soon as we then assembled to watch, however, the image would promptly return to snow, sending us back to our command posts for another try. And so it went evening after evening. With such adversity, I lost all interest in two-week-old TV. Reading was far more gratifying — not to mention more reliable.

On weekends, we frequently went to the movies showing at one of the two movie houses in Juneau — the 20th Century on Front Street and the Capitol on Franklin. Standard fare was westerns punctuated by an occasional World War II movie. My family distained musicals. Besides books, movies offered one of the few transcendent experiences to a young child. I remember as a small child often thinking about God, in whom I was supposed to believe, and wondering what would lead me to truly know that God existed. Certainly, a miracle would do the trick. Thus, when "The Miracle of Our Lady of Fatima," my first religious film, came to the 20th Century Theater, I had high expectations. I remember afterwards, standing outside, sorely disappointed that the answer was not forthcoming.

Our family loved picnics. On the weekends, we often invited neighbors or friends, packed up our meal and drove up the canyon carved by Montana Creek, an area deserted except for an occasional trout fisherman. There we built a fire, cooked out, waded and played in the stream, visited and lounged for the afternoon.

Vacations were not part of life until I reached age thirteen. Then my parents decided to make their first trip out of Juneau to pick up a new, red Chevrolet station wagon. My mother, Alan, Lynn, and I flew to El Paso, Texas, to spend a week with my Aunt Hivana and family, who lived in nearby Las Cruces. Summer in New Mexico was hot, and the swimming pools were crowded. My brother, sister, and I stood out in the crowd for our pale, white skin, causing my aunt to worry that we were anemic.

Montana Creek.

My father then joined us and we started the three-thousand-mile trip north, stopping to view many bridges along the way, given my father's interest in engineering. Mid-way we stopped in Yellowstone National Park and then proceeded north to the famed Alcan Highway, the only road connection between Alaska and the continental United States, built in 1943 as part of the US defense against Japan. Barely ten years old at the time, the Alcan was then unpaved. We were fortunate to have dry weather because the road famously became impassable in the rain. We drove for hours and hours without seeing a sign of human life. At night, we "camped," my mother, Lynn, and I sleeping in the car. Alan remembers himself and dad sleeping under the car in our Army surplus, mummy-style sleeping bags. Everyone remembers the mosquitoes, which are the stuff of legends — out-sized, ubiquitous and voracious. At over a thousand miles, the Alcan took several days of driving, eventually delivering us Whitehorse, Yukon Territory where we turned south to Haines and caught the small car ferry for the six-hour trip home to Juneau.

Our second vacation came a year or two later when we took the ferry to Haines and then drove north to Anchorage and Fairbanks. We all agreed that Anchorage seemed unremarkable, just another big town. We passed up Mt. McKinley (now Denali) National Park and headed to Fairbanks, arriving on June 21st, the longest day of the year. This inspired us to drive north for another hundred and fifty miles to Circle City on the Artic Circle. There we joined other families spending the night camped on a hill watching the sun circumnavigate the horizon, never touching down. The experience was about as exciting as watching the grass grow.

We always kept a boat on the bay. First it was an extremely seaworthy, round-bottom, sixteen-foot skiff powered by a twenty-horsepower Mercury outboard. Later it was a twenty-foot cabin cruiser called *The Wolf*, with a comedic depiction of a wolf on the bow, powered by a seventy-horsepower Mercury outboard motor. We used the boat for weekend fishing and picnicking on the uninhabited Coughlin and Portland Islands in the middle of Auke Bay.

Guns were as common as can openers in Auke Bay. A loaded pistol resided in the top drawer of my parents' bed table (never mind that we never locked the front door), and rifles always hung from racks in our living room. When I was twelve, my father took me by boat to Portland Island, the largest and most distant island in Auke Bay, which was deserted and had a long expanse of beach where I learned to shoot.

I fear I was a disappointment. The rifle had such a powerful recoil that I mostly focused on how not to bruise my shoulder, rather than how to hit the target. Later, I learned that several of my friends had been taught to shoot in exactly the same setting and manner — by their fathers on one of these islands. Then, when Juneau built Harborview, the new elementary school in 1952, they built a rifle range in the basement, and I, like all my friends, joined the rifle club. I proudly sewed the insignia of the Junior National Rifle Association on my jacket. Guns were not politicized in those days and it is hard for present-day urbanites and middle-class people to understand how much guns are part of the

Dad and mom fishing from our skiff.

warp and woof of American rural culture, especially on the frontier.

Shortly after we moved into our new house by the lake, the US Department of the Interior offered ninety-nine-year leases to build hunting cabins on Admiralty Island, the ninety-mile-long island roughly twenty miles straight across Lynn Canal from Auke Bay. We joined with another family, the Tickell's, to lease beachfront land and to build a primitive, one-room hunting cabin. (The Department of Interior promptly reversed itself, deciding that the land should remain wilderness, and has been trying to get the land back ever since.) Admiralty is overwhelmingly national forest, largely deserted and noted for its very high brown bear population. Once built, we would go to enjoy weekends there in seclusion, as though Auke Bay wasn't secluded enough already. These occasions were far more fun for me when I could invite my friends, usually Louise, to join.

The waterways in southeastern Alaska can be treacherous and unpredictable, to say the least. My father had temporarily swapped our more seaworthy skiff for a similarly-sized, flat-bottomed boat owned by the Bureau of Public Roads, when we decided to go to our hunting cabin one weekend. The weather was good when we went but became a margin call when we started

Dad and Alan, picking up *The Wolf* from Juneau.

back on Sunday. Once we started, however, the winds began to pick up and storm clouds continued to gather. In bad weather, wind and waves howl undeterred down the hundred-mile length of Lynn Canal from Skagway in the north, past Juneau in the south.

In rough weather, you always want to take the waves from the bow, but crossing Lynn Canal meant being pummeled from the side. A flat-bottomed boat is the least stable and the hardest to handle. The force of a wave would pitch us into the air and then drop us into the trough, the boat shuddering as the wave crashed over us. The further we went, the fiercer became the wind and waves, but turning back quickly became more dangerous than plowing forward. So, we cut a long diagonal course north, slowing down to soften the blow of the waves. As wave after wave smashed against our boat, my mother bailed furiously while my father struggled to keep the bow pointed into the waves.

We all wore life jackets and my parents placed my brother and me and our Labrador retriever, Windy (my sister had not yet been born), under the half-covered bow, where we could not see the waves coming but could feel and hear the boat being slammed and doused, lifted and dropped, time after time. We were terrified that each wave would be our last and we would be thrown into the furious and frigid waters of the canal. After hours of hand-to-hand combat, fear, and adrenalin, we finally made it to the sheltered waters of Auke Bay, our diagonal course having landed us miles north from where we started. Years later, the incident came up in conversation with my mother who expressed total surprise that we had remembered and been aware of the danger. I thought to myself, "we may have been young, but we surely weren't dumb."

Dad: Working in the Bush

The move to our new house in 1953, when I was ten years old, marked a new chapter of family life. By now my parents had made it securely into the middle class. The earlier challenges — moving, getting established, building houses, climbing the bootstrap — while difficult, had drawn our family together and provided some of the most stable and happy years of family life. Shortly after we completed our new house, however, the nature of my father's work began to change. Increasingly, he led crews into the wilderness to survey for roads, most of which would never be built. The sites were remote and reachable only by boat or seaplane. He and his crew would set up camp and be gone for weeks, if not months, at a time with little or no communication possible. I don't know whether the attraction for my father was positive pull —

outdoorsmanship, working and living in nature, male companionship, liberty and adventure — or negative push, perhaps difficulties in his relationship with my mother. Or perhaps it was just his natural restlessness.

We all hated his absences, but no one more than my mother. She would go into a serious, days-long funk whenever he announced a new assignment or the extension of an old one. No doubt the situation called up the many abandonments of her early childhood and doubts about her own worth. My father's growing absences threw the two into conflict, often fueled by alcohol. She began to suffer spells of deep depression in which she could be bitter, aggressive and irrational toward all. During a fight, she would suddenly bolt and drive off unannounced in the car, wheels screeching, causing me to worry about an accident or suicide. These fights instilled in me fear, despair, and confusion and I would oscillate between the desire to defend and protect first one parent and then the other. One afternoon Alan and I returned from school to find my mother curled up in a fetal position on the floor of their closet. I was aghast, frightened for her and for our family and angry at feeling a responsibility I could not assume. To compound the situation, I'm sure that my own growing adolescent need for separation and independence felt to her like yet another abandonment.

My father's work in the bush was seasonal and he hired many college students in the summers. I could get a job for any of my (male) friends by simply mentioning them to my father. Flying back to Juneau for our fiftieth high school reunion, I sat beside a man slightly younger than me, who lived in Juneau. As we began to talk, he mentioned working as a civil engineer, which led me to mention my father. Yes, he remembered my father distinctly. He had worked for him as a college student and that was his introduction to engineering. Then he said something curious. "Bill was famous for being a fast talker." I was perplexed, thinking "How strange," since it couldn't be further from how I would describe my father. When I probed, however, I discovered that I had misunderstood. He was famous for being a "fast walker" and this was indeed true. He could out-walk anyone of any age, whether on a sidewalk or traversing the most rugged Alaskan wilderness. His assistant and close friend, a younger man named Jim Nelson, reported panting to keep up with my dad while leaving the young college guys straggling many yards behind.

Among the young men he hired was my best friend Louise's brother, Loren Howerter. Loren told me in later life that he became an engineer because of my father. Loren was smart and hard-working but, coming from a poor family, he had little vision of going to college. My father encouraged him, sitting down with him to help fill out college and financial applications. Loren got his engineering degree at the University of Alaska, travelled the world as an oil platform engineer, and had a very successful career. I had no idea.

The work took a toll on my dad in later life. Work in the bush was accessible only by boat or seaplane (at best) and both are subject to Alaska's rough and unpredictable weather. The longer he did this work, the more frightened he became of flying. One day while being lifted from a remote work site in the interior of Alaska by helicopter, he asked the pilot what would happen if the helicopter's one and only engine failed. The pilot (apparently a man of few words) responded by cutting the engine. It turns out that the helicopter's rotors are angled such that, as the plane falls, they counter-rotate, creating a gentle counter-lift and slowing its descent. I don't believe the pilot took this demonstration to its full conclusion. Years after retirement, my father and my mother flew out to visit me and my family in New York. I had not seen him in a couple of years and was shocked at what I thought was his deterioration, marked by the shaking of his hands. Had he developed Parkinson's? A day later, however, the palsy had disappeared. Neither years nor even a mammoth 747 jet could abate his fear of flying.

Family Politics

My parents were a mass of political contradictions. Both were conservative, and I believed them to be life-long Republicans, with their own personal experience serving as the touchstone. My mother was the more conservative, believing, for instance, that President Roosevelt had conspired in the Pearl Harbor attack for the purpose of involving the United States in World War II. They valued education, individualism, industry, and independence, asking no favors and taking no handouts. Most formative was their own experience of the American Dream — starting with nothing, working hard, taking risks, and making it solidly into the middle class. They believed that, if they could do it with hard work and enterprise, so could anyone.

Their personal values of independence and self-sufficiency did not extend to Alaska when it came to statehood, however. As a territory, Alaska received considerable financial benefits from the federal government. Unlike the majority, my parents felt no pride in statehood and saw no reason why Alaska should give up its territorial benefits. On July 4, 1959, following Eisenhower's earlier signing of the Alaska Statehood Act, Juneau went wild in celebration. Feelings about statehood notwithstanding, we joined the crowds to watch the most amazing show of fireworks ever.

My father read the paper, was reasonably well-informed and had opinions on many subjects. His reaction to the passage of the Communist Control Act of 1954, criminalizing membership in the Communist Party, struck me. He found out about it upon returning from a hunting trip on Admiralty Island. He stormed into the house in a rant, asking rhetorically, "What day will I come home from the cabin and find that I'm a criminal because of what I believe or what organization I belong to?" His reaction stemmed not from progressive leanings but from a position of personal liberty, the role of government and basic sense of fairness.

In 1964 my parents voted for Barry Goldwater, the arch-conservative Republican candidate for president, and Ernest Gruening, the early and ardent Democratic opponent of the Vietnam War, for US Senate. For them, this was no contradiction. Everything translated into practicality — how would it affect us and our ability to get along as a family? They were no ideologues. As long as Gruening delivered to Alaskans, they could care less his position on a far-off war. In fact, they, as many Alaskans, often admired a maverick. Later, when Alan enlisted in the Army ahead of the draft, the Vietnam War would not have been far-off and they would have cared deeply.

My mother's political views were more emotionally-based and less informed than my father's. Thus, it was probably FDR's responsibility for the possible loss of my father during World War II that gained him her enmity more than a matter of facts or world view. She reacted similarly when I later became active in the civil rights movement, less out of political disagreement than fear for my safety, displeasure at my having stepped off the graduate student track, and the feeling that I was being presumptuous, if not grandiose, to think that I could affect national events.

On his deathbed, my father revealed to me that he had always leaned Democratic and was a supporter of the New Deal and an admirer of the Kennedys. I don't believe that my mother ever knew that, over their lifetimes, he had consistently cancelled out her Republican vote. He was nothing if not an avoider of conflict.

Much later, when she was in her late seventies, on an impulse, my mother became a Democrat. Republican as she might be, her dislike and distain for George W.

Bush knew no bounds. In her eyes, he was an ignorant, spoiled brat, born with a silver spoon in his mouth, the antithesis of everything she experienced and stood for. Living alone in Las Vegas, the time came to renew her driver's license. With great pride and by herself, she plotted and executed the drive to the DMV office, arriving an hour before opening. DMV workers took mercy and invited her to sit inside as the desert sun ascended. Nevada had a motor-voter law and officials must have asked her if she was registered to vote and did she want to change her party affiliation? My mother spotted the opportunity. She walked out of the DMV that morning, the proud owner of a renewed driver's license and a Democratic Party membership card.

Chapel-by-the-Lake: New Vistas

When I was twelve years old, Ken and Betty Smith moved to Auke Bay to take over the ministry of our community church, the Chapel-by-the-Lake. Ken was young and dynamic, and particularly dedicated to young people. He once commented that "to influence a young person is to influence a lifetime," and there is no example better than my own. The Chapel was one of the few social institutions in Auke Bay and it was accessible by walking. Ken quickly established junior high and senior high youth groups of around

Chapel-by-the-Lake (left) and the view outside (right).

a dozen kids each — called Westminster Fellowship or "WF." The WF groups met on Sunday evenings for thoughtful discussions, followed by games and refreshments. Because homes in Auke Bay were far flung, Ken would drive members home after meetings. Some of the best discussions took place in his station wagon, and members vied for who would be delivered home last.

Aside from regular Sunday night meetings, WF engaged in both service projects and fun activities. We must have hiked every charted trail in the Juneau area; we had swimming parties and skating parties; we went to movies; we trick-or-treated for UNICEF; we conducted "progressive" dinners, eating one course at each member's house; we went Christmas caroling; we played silly and riotous games. We collected roadside trash, worked on construction of the new Christian education building, conducted a church service once a year and helped Auke Bay families in need. We wrote follow-up cards to tourists who visited our picturesque log Chapel overlooking Auke Lake and Mendenhall Glacier, resulting in a steady stream of contributions.

Our WF group organized a benefit — a spaghetti dinner — to raise money to send Lee Hagmeier, the fellow-WFer who had been blinded and nearly killed in a surprise encounter with a brown bear, to the Perkins Institute for the Blind. The community outpouring was so massive as to be overwhelming. To serve,

Intial WF Group: John Hagmeir, Loren Howerter, JoAn Lynch, me, Louise Howerter.

the entire manse became our kitchen and its basement, our dining room. I seem to remember the manse bathtub filled with spaghetti, truckloads of bread to be buttered and garlicked, and spaghetti sauce everywhere. Betty, the minister's wife, remembers finding spaghetti in her newborn daughter's bassinette the next day. The undertaking was so immense that it giddily reduced us to giggles as the night wore on. I don't remember how much money we raised.

Ann Coleman, 1950s.

My parents were not particularly religious. They believed in God, but more in action than in faith. My mother hated church services (more specifically, anyone preaching at her) but nevertheless served as treasurer of the Chapel for many years and sporadically attended Bible study. My father worked to help build the Chapel but appeared in church only on Easter and Christmas. They later joined the Chapel square-dancing group.

WF began to introduce me to the outside world. As a service project, I spent my sophomore year reading the *New York Times* to Ann Coleman, a self-educated nonagenarian and founder of the Juneau Public Library, now blind and living alone on Fritz Cove Road. She was a powerful intellect. I had never heard of the *New York Times* nor had I a clue about politics. I would not have known a conservative from a liberal, so remote was politics from our lives. As I read, she provided me the context and background to the issues, editorialized, and engaged me in discussion, conveying the expectation that I should be knowledgeable and have opinions. I was surprised at the immediacy of world and national events to her and was taken aback to hear her refer to JFK as "Jack," as if he was a personal friend. She gave me a glimpse of literary and political sophistication and engagement that I did not even know existed.

Much as I loved Alaska and thought I could never leave it, life in Auke Bay was provincial and the horizons narrow. High school was a social wasteland. I knew that I was smart but suffered the quintessential adolescent curse of feeling I did not fit in — not with the smart kids, not with the popular kids, not with anyone, it seemed. I didn't understand the art of flirting nor the need to hide my intelligence or competence, making me feel doomed to failure when it came to boys. Living "out the road," resulted in limited accessibility to friends and social activities. Jobs available to adolescents were boring and dead-ended. Kind and generous as our neighbors were, I could see no one whose life or career I wanted to emulate. Home life frequently felt bleak and turbulent. Surely, I felt, there must be more to life than this.

In this context, I became a sponge soaking up any trace of deeper meaning or broader purpose, and the Chapel, the WF group, and the attention of Ken and Betty ministered to that need. I pulled in as close as I could. I babysat for their growing family, which seemed happy compared to my own; I worked every Saturday as the church janitor; I taught Sunday School and

Reverend Ken Smith and his wife Betty in the 1950s.

Vacation Bible School; I volunteered whenever I could. I was flattered to be asked to host a visiting delegation of Presbyterian officials on a site-seeing tour of Juneau and environs. Attending Rainbow Glacier Camp, the Presbyterian camp located outside of Haines — a full day's cruise on any of the church's three ships from Auke Bay — widened my horizons, inspired me and permanently replaced Girl Scout Camp as the highlight of my summers.

Perhaps the power of Ken and Betty's influence lay in making me feel special — as though I had special abilities and some special destiny. Every child needs to feel special — a need that rarely can be met by parents whose role requires them to consider their progeny special. And through the church, the Smiths revealed to me abilities I didn't even know I had. For example, Rainbow Glacier Camp brought together young people from all the Southeastern Alaska towns and villages, year after year, fostering a network of friendships among the most active church-going youths. Ken helped to constitute us as the "Youth Presbytery" (the youthful analog to the geographical governing unit of the church) of which I was an officer. At his urging, I became the co-editor of a newsletter called "YAP" (Youth of Alaska Presbytery), something I never would have imagined myself doing. I began to see that I could act as an agent, not just a passive participant in my own life.

The crowning event of my adolescence was the summer of 1958, spent aboard the *Anna Jackman*, the sixty-foot "queen of the Presbyterian navy" which, along with its sister ships the SJS (Sheldon Jackson School) II and the Princeton Hall, ministered to Native villages, logging camps and other remote outposts of Southeastern Alaska. Although I was only a high school junior, Ken had me included in a group of

Summer, 1958, I spent on the *Anna Jackman* as part of a Vacation Bible School ministry.

college students recruited each summer from across the country to teach Vacation Bible School throughout Southeastern Alaska. The experience was magical. I was flattered to be accepted and pleased to find that I could hold my own among older and more sophisticated college students. My team was assigned to the *Anna Jackman* and I got to know and admire its permanent residents: the skipper, Dick Nelson, and his family. I loved meeting the people and getting to know these remote communities that had previously been only names or dots on a map.

Living on a boat is a culture of its own, filled with its own language and customs, adventures, and peculiarities. These included awaking at four-thirty one morning to see one of the lowest tides of the year and discovering exotic sea life I had never seen before. One afternoon we docked in Wrangell and all disembarked to go to a movie. When we returned in the evening, we found the tide had gone out and the boat was now twenty feet below dock level, reachable only by climbing down a slippery, barnacled and seaweed-encrusted vertical ladder in the dark. I loved every moment of it. The summer ended in a workcamp at Sheldon Jackson, a residential junior college located in Sitka and operated by the Presbyterian Church for Native Alaskans, where for two weeks we painted

Ronda at Workcamp, Sheldon Jackson Junior College.

dorm rooms, faculty houses, and everything else in our path. Finally, there followed a leadership training program at Rainbow Glacier Camp. I was honored to be considered a candidate for leadership. I was rapidly acquiring the vision that, yes indeed, there could be more to life.

Summer Jobs

Need I say again that our family had a deep work ethic? One of the most devastating charges that could be levelled against a person was that he or she was "lazy." Struggling up the bootstrap was a family affair and we were members of the team. No one told me I had to work. No one had to. At home, I did whatever I could, helping with dinner, setting the table, washing dishes, baking, washing clothes, ironing, gardening, picking berries, making jam, and whatever else I could contribute. I started working outside our home from the earliest possible age, initially babysitting for neighbors on evenings and weekends.

My first full-time summer job was scrubbing school buses for the Lindegards, the family who owned and operated the local school bus company. Their base of operations, including their home and the bus garage, were located about a quarter mile toward the Bay from us. Eric Lindegard handled maintenance and mechanics and was one of the kindest men I had ever met. His wife Myrtle conducted the business end and supervised the cleaning. She had a community-wide reputation for being tough as nails and appeared to have had few friends. My mother warned me that, if I could work successfully for her, I could work for anyone.

Another boy and I formed a crew of two, and we scraped, scrubbed, and polished every square inch of the bus fleet, which then numbered about six buses, inside and out. By the time we finished, you could have comfortably eaten your dinner off of any surface on the entire bus. Not a single speck went unnoticed. My stance toward Myrtle Lindegard was to work hard, keep my head low, never indulge in unrelated conversation, and always be deferential. While demanding, she was also fair, she paid reasonably well, and she came to trust, if not like, me. I was pleased with my success. I banked my money and at the end of the summer I treated myself to a 35mm Tower camera from Sears Roebuck.

On Saturdays, I worked as the church janitor, dusting, vacuuming, polishing, cleaning windows and scrubbing bathrooms. After school, I laid out ads for the local newspaper, the *Daily Alaska Empire*. I tried my hand at domestic work, cleaning the house of a neighbor, the Druxman's. She had been my beloved second grade teacher and he was a real estate agent. She was away for the summer, so I cleaned, washed and polished floors, changed beds, scrubbed bathrooms and sundry other household tasks, with virtually no attention or guidance from him. This was the only job from which I ever got fired. I had no idea what he expected, and it felt unfair.

As I grew older I held a series of summer jobs with the Alaska State Employment Security Department. As the State capitol, Juneau hosted a welter of government offices, a rich source of clerical summer jobs for students. All roads to those well-paying summer jobs ran through Amanda Cook, our high school typing and shorthand teacher. Those offices all turned to her for summer workers and her recommendation could make or break a summer job opportunity. Miss Cook was a tall, middle-aged, single woman, with a reputation for being rigid; a typing fanatic, she was the kind of teacher who invites jokes and pranks from her students, which we readily supplied. I suspect she had little else going on in her life. A strikeover was beyond an unforgivable sin, and improper form in front of the typewriter could land you in purgatory. Her pinnacle experience was having visited a former student many years later and spying the typing manual on her coffee table. Typing was her be-all and end-all. As a student, the kiss of death was letting her know that you already knew how to type, which I did. You would then certainly have developed terrible habits, which would have to be unlearned before you could start from scratch and learn the right way from her.

So, wanting a good summer job, I enrolled in first-year typing and never said a word even though I could already type sixty words a minute. I patiently typed every exercise, no matter how simple and repetitive, took every test, and did every piece of homework. At about week three, Mrs. Cook towered over me and my typewriter, complimented my talent, and suggested promoting me to the second-year class. Yes! I innately understood that she needed to own my success. I didn't. All I needed was a good summer job. I graduated that class typing over a hundred words a minute and got the cream-of-the-crop summer jobs through the rest of high school and college. Typing is still my most proficient skill and the experience was an important life lesson in strategies for getting what you want.

My exciting summer on the *Anna Jackman* contrasted starkly with my summer job experiences before and after. Typical was the next summer, which I spent in the Commissioner's office of the Alaska Employment Security Administration, transcribing verbatim a single hearing in a single disputed unemployment case. The following year, I worked for the Investigations Unit, where my entire job for three months consisted of typing onto form letters and envelopes the thousands upon thousands of employer addresses, employee names, and social security numbers from a massive computer print-out, produced by the earliest generation of computers. A year later, the computer would have mastered my job as well. Such excruciating boredom was an interesting, if torturous, lesson in self-knowledge. I soon withdrew from my surroundings into the labyrinth of my own mind where I invented, lived and relived elaborate fantasies, all with me as the unlikely hero. My coworkers felt sorry for me and would stop by to chat and offer diversion, but soon enough I just wanted to be left alone to romp in my made-up fantasy world. At the end of the summer the big boss, whom I could see through the glass window of his office, asked me to format a small dataset for presentation. I organized it into a simple grid and he was bowled over at my "brilliance," as was his boss. To myself I thought, "What they don't know." That summer fired in me a burning resolve to find a future life of interest and meaning, regardless of all else. I would rather be selling pencils on the street corner than face a life of such tortured monotony.

I was interested in social work as a career and was delighted during my final college summer to land a job as a social work trainee in the Juneau office of the federal Bureau of Indian Affairs, where I assisted in case work for Native Alaskan families. A trip to the tiny village of Hoonah produced a quintessential Alaskan airplane experience. Located on the otherwise uninhabited Chichagof island, Hoonah was serviced by a six-seat Alaska Coastal Airlines amphibious seaplane. Leaving the village with three passengers that afternoon, the plane pulled onto the gravel runway and taxied down to the end and then mysteriously stopped, waiting twenty minutes for no one knew what. With only two planes a day, it was most assuredly not air traffic. Finally, an old red pickup came careening down the runway, clouds of dust arising behind it, and pulled up beside the plane. The driver jerked to a stop, jumped out of the cab and handed a large king salmon up to the pilot through his side window. And with that, the pilot revved the engine and we took off.

Toward the end of the summer, I met a friend's mother on the street. My friend was enrolled at Antioch College, noted for integrating work experience with academic learning. While her mother barely knew me, I suddenly found her intensely interested in my job. Finally, she mentioned that she was scouting jobs for Antioch and was going to recommend that my job be incorporated into its work-study program. Irritated at feeling invisible, I responded, "You mean so that this job would not be available to Alaskan kids like me?" She stammered with surprise. Apparently, it never dawned on her that the young person with whom she was conversing might have feelings. I think in the end, she backed off.

Each payday I would treat myself to a book, thoroughly pre-browsed over the preceding two weeks in our one bookstore, and usually on a spiritual, philosophical, or theological topic. I faithfully deposited the rest of my paycheck into my savings account, which was held jointly with my dad, with the objective of paying as much as I could toward college expenses. He handled my college arrangements however and, when I graduated from college, I found that he had removed nothing from my bank account. My education was my parents' gift to me and my bank account became a nest egg for the future.

Leaving Alaska

The summer of my third college year was my last in Auke Bay and with my family. One fall morning, at four o'clock, I left on the *Alaska Marine Highway*, the ferry that serves as a highway to all the otherwise inaccessible, small Southeastern Alaskan towns and links to Canadian ferries connecting to Vancouver and Seattle. Despite the early morning hour and the fifteen-mile drive, Ken Smith joined my parents in seeing me off. A potent mix of anxiety, excitement, loneliness, nostalgia, love, and gratitude welled up in my chest as the motors shuddered to life, the pilot put the engine into gear and, with the surge of the propellers, we pulled away from the dock and Juneau began to recede in the early morning light. All I knew was that, whatever chapters were to follow, they would be nothing like the chapter that I had just closed.

EPILOGUE

Ronda

My adolescent experience with the church led me to choose Lewis and Clark College in Portland, Oregon, a small (fifteen hundred students), liberal arts college, then loosely affiliated with the Presbyterian Church. It turned out to be an excellent choice. Many of my peers went to the University of Washington, where many became lost souls in a sea of twenty-five thousand students — fully two and a half times more than all the people who lived in the Juneau of our childhood. By contrast, Lewis and Clark was a friendly, supportive place. A school representative met me at the airport when I first arrived, and the Assistant to the President looked out for the small handful of Alaskan students, inviting us to dinner and assuring we were taken care of during school vacations, since we could not easily return home. Lewis and Clark offered a halfway house and nurturing spring board out into a big, wide world that I had never known.

While I consider myself deeply spiritual, I have not turned out to be a religious person, nor do I participate in organized religion, which no doubt deeply disappointed Ken and Betty Smith. The values I took from my early church experience, however, are deeply embedded and have guided my subsequent path in life. Among the most important are: that every person, regardless of race, color, creed, or class, is equally precious and deserving in the eyes of God; and that, if you truly believe in something, you must act; you must dedicate yourself; you must let it shape your life.

Had I grown up in the aftermath of the women's movement, in addition to retaining my maiden name, I almost certainly would have opted for the ministry, but in the early 1960s, that male-bastion was a reach too far. The alternative for women was Christian Education, but why would I ever strive to be second best? I knew that I simply wanted to make a difference and to help people, so I decided on a career as a counsellor, following the role model that Ken (and the ministry in part) offered.

Upon graduation from Lewis and Clark, I received a fully paid doctoral scholarship to Vanderbilt University's Department of Psychology. The year was 1965 and the civil rights movement was in full bloom. Not having to work that summer and being curious,

I decided to embark on one last summer fling, one that would prove to be a life-altering experience — a civil rights related summer project sponsored by the Presbyterian Church in the majority-Black counties of Amelia and Nottaway, Virginia, south of Richmond. I joined a diverse team of some ten college students who, in the mornings, taught Vacation Bible School in two rural Black Presbyterian churches and, in the afternoons, registered voters. We worked side-by-side with two civil rights groups: the Virginia Student Civil Rights Committee (VSCRC), organized by students at the University of Virginia, and a student group sponsored by SCOPE (Summer Community Organization and Political Education), a project of the Southern Christian Leadership Conference (SCLC). Ironically in hindsight, the hot voting issue was election of representatives to the county Tobacco Board which, under federal price supports, determined the apportionment of land each farmer received for this critical, cash-producing crop.

Never had I imagined the poverty, discrimination, hatred, and danger that were the stuff of everyday life for these rural, Black Virginians. The Klan was active in Southside Virginia, holding several rallies that summer. In a drive-by shooting one evening, a bullet grazed the head of one local activist, teaching us to never stand in silhouette. One mid-summer afternoon in the living room of one of Amelia County's civil rights stalwarts, we sat riveted to the TV as President Johnson signed into law the federal Voting Rights Act. The times were electric. We could see history being made before our eyes and we could feel that we were an important part of that change. When the Presbyterian project ended early in the summer, I moved over to working with VSCRC.

By September, I had lost my appetite for clinical psychology and the one-on-one approach to helping people. Having been exposed to grave injustice and the fight against it, I experienced myself for the first time as a potential agent of far more sweeping and fundamental change. After a half-hearted try at graduate school, and to the despair of the faculty and my family, I dropped out to work the following two years for a newly-formed civil-rights group, the Southern Student Organizing Committee (SSOC), the group most closely related to VSCRC.

In the fifty years that have followed, I have been showered with blessings, largely attributable to the values so early instilled in me by my parents, Ken and Betty Smith, and the church. I met my husband-to-be, David Kotelchuck, in the civil rights movement in Nashville, and for the last fifty years we have shared our

Dave and Ronda Kotelchuck.

dedication to each other, to family, and to social justice. We settled in New York City and have been blessed with jobs filled with purpose and challenge, in which we could feel that we were genuinely a force for change. I worked for a crusading health policy organization, the City's public hospital system, and eventually was asked to lead a new nonprofit organization — the Primary Care Development Corporation — dedicated to bringing the most basic health care to communities that would otherwise lack it.

I have been blessed with leadership opportunities, for which, as a young person, I would never have guessed myself qualified. I am blessed not only with a wonderful husband and his large and loving extended family, but with two amazing daughters, Tamar and Shana, who have adapted their own versions of our values and who now have their own families, including our three grandchildren. The common thread that runs through and binds together these many years is that of social justice and giving back in return for the many privileges with which I have been blessed — living one's faith and beliefs. Both Dave and I are now retired.

My Siblings

Five years younger than me, my brother Alan attended Montana State University, getting his degree in civil engineering in 1970. Shortly thereafter he enlisted in the Army ahead of the draft and missed being sent to Vietnam by a fluke, instead spending two years guarding the war criminal Rudolf Hess, who was then imprisoned in Berlin's Spandau Prison. He returned to earn his master's degree in engineering at Oregon State

University in 1974, worked as a soils engineer in Montana and Utah, met his wife-to-be, Pat, married, lived and worked in Las Vegas where their two daughters, Megan and Dana, were born. The family moved to Reno in 1999 where, after ten years, he retired.

Alan Stilley.

Three siblings, Lynn, Alan and Ronda.

My sister Lynn, 13 years younger than me, attended the University of Puget Sound in Seattle, graduating in 1974. She moved to San Francisco to attend graduate school but, while on vacation, met and later married a man from Virgin Gorda in the British Virgin Islands. She lived

Lynn Stilley.

there for ten years, during which she gave birth to her daughter, Jeannette Wheatley. She later divorced and moved to Las Vegas to raise her daughter, earn a master's degree in marriage and family therapy and develop a specialty in treating gambling addiction. She still lives in Las Vegas and maintains a private practice. Her daughter lives in Seattle.

My Parents
During the early 1960s, my parents purchased the Nugget Shop with friends Jim and Ruth Nelson. Founded by Belle Simpson, the storied grand dame of Juneau, the Shop carried expensive gold and hand-carved ivory jewelry, hand-sewn parkas and moccasins and original oil paintings by Sidney Lawrence, the famous Alaskan artist, along with all the usual

tourist trinkets. My mother managed the shop, which sat at Second and Seward Streets, one of the main intersections of downtown Juneau, while my father continued working as a civil engineer. After ten years, they liquidated the store and my mother then went to work briefly for one of the State agencies.

My father and his closest colleagues left the Bureau of Public Roads in the early 1960s due to a conflict of interest. They set up a private engineering firm — Wyller, Killowich, Van Doren & Hazard — where he worked until 1972 when it was purchased by an Anchorage firm. By now, my parents were middle-aged. Alaska is a difficult place in which to

The storied Nugget Shop, was purchased by my parents in the 1960s.

My parents relocated to Coos Bay, Oregon in 1974 and purchased the Bridge Bay Motel.

grow old. Moreover, my father — now unemployed and at home — was drinking more than ever. To my mother, this added up to a dead end and thus she, in her abiding strength, decided that they should leave Alaska. They purchased the Bay Bridge Motel in Coos Bay, Oregon, in 1974, sold our house and left after twenty-four eventful years. My father died in 1979 of a massive heart attack, I believe in grief over the loss of his earlier purpose-driven, adventurous, outdoor life in Alaska. In 1984, my mother moved to Las Vegas to be with and help my brother's and sister's young families. She died there of lung cancer in 2007.

My Friends

Louise Howerter became a grade school teacher in Kodiak, Alaska, after attending Mississippi State College for Women and the University of Alaska. She married Pete Jackson, a biologist who worked for the Alaska State Department of Fish and Game. Retiring after twenty years, Louise and Pete moved to Squim,

Louise Howerter Jackson.

Washington, on the Olympic Peninsula. She died following a ten-year struggle with breast cancer.

JoAn Lynch moved with her family to Eugene, Oregon, in our eighth-grade year and attended the

JoAn Lynch Mauer.

University of Oregon, getting her degree in journalism. She lived and worked in Southern California and eventually moved to Vancouver, BC, where she worked in human resources. There she met and married Michel Maurer and raised her daughter, Nathalie. We still maintain a close friendship.

Ken and Betty Smith in later years.

My Mentors

Ken and Betty Smith served the Chapel-by-the-Lake for some twenty years. They subsequently took a church in Waimea, Hawaii, where they served for many years. They returned to Alaska to minister to a church in Wasilla, outside of Anchorage, before retiring and moving first to Surprise, Arizona, and then to Ferndale, Washington. Ken died of complications following a fall in 2017 at the age of 92. Betty continues to live in Ferndale. We have remained in touch over the years and I remain grateful for the role they played in my life.

Juneau and Auke Bay

The town of Juneau has grown from ten thousand in the 1950s to roughly thirty thousand now. Squeezed between Gastineau Channel, Mt. Juneau, and Mt. Roberts, population growth has pushed the City out into Glacier Valley, Auke Bay, and Douglas Island. Downtown sports several major office buildings and, at the heart of the old business district, the Sealaska Heritage Institute has opened, honoring the culture of the indigenous Tlingit and Haida tribes. A tram now takes observers up high on Mt. Roberts, a mountain once accessible only by a steep, half-day climb.

Over the last fifty years, Mendenhall Glacier has retreated and shrunken to but a semblance of its former self under the onslaught of global warming. Glacier Valley, the largely deserted wilderness of my youth, is the area's new population center and is filling up with suburban development, including tract housing, schools, and shopping malls. Juneau even has a Walmart. Auke Bay now hosts the University of Alaska Southeast (UASE), located on the shore of Auke Lake along the deserted and wooded short-cut (called "Spur Road") that, as kids, we once used to reach the Chapel-by-the-Lake. The log chapel has been joined by a Christian Education building, built when I was a teenager, and a much larger sanctuary. A trail

Mendenhall Glacier in 1958 (above) and in 2012 (below).
Disappearing under the onslaught of global warming.

(Credit, top image: M.T. Millett, National Snow and Ice Data Center (NSIDC)
(Credit, bottom image: Matthew J. Beedle)

built on the deserted, back-side of Auke Lake now makes entire circumference accessible. The wilderness behind our house has given way to a road to the UASE dormitories. The house my parents built is now over sixty years old and the two small spruce trees we planted when we moved in have grown so large as to nearly obscure the house and its wonderous view of Auke Lake. On my last two visits, the house was vacant and for sale where — priced at an astonishing $1 million — it is likely to remain.

Auke Bay now has a mail delivery, bus service, centralized water and sewer systems, fire hydrants, and paved roads, often lined by sidewalks, which still cause me to do a double-take. Phones — both cell phones and land lines — as well as TV are as common as anywhere else in the United States and cable service precludes families from wandering around their yards holding TV antennae in search of a signal. Several schools now serve Glacier Valley and I notice that children now play football, baseball, and soccer in addition to basketball. Juneau has developed a small symphony orchestra.

Nature and the wilderness remain very close at hand, and swaths that were inaccessible to us as children have now been opened to trails and roads. I am happy that life is easier and more "normal" for Auke Bay's current residents and constantly amazed at the contrast with the pioneering conditions of my youth. I'm also slightly wistful that those who remember those earlier times grow fewer and fewer. Saddest of all, however, the friends of my parents — the older generation who formed such a tight community — are by now nearly all gone.

I remain close to many of my elementary and high school classmates. Turnover in Juneau was low and there came to be about a hundred of us in our grade. Whether we liked each other or not, over twelve years we grew to know each other well. Our class is unusually cohesive, and we maintain an active listserv that keeps us abreast of each other and developments in Juneau. We hold class reunions every five years, with the even years taking place in Juneau and the odd years in Seattle, where so many Alaskans eventually settle. Some fifteen members of the Girl Scout troop also maintain a separate network. We commit ourselves to a written update twice a year, and in the interim communication is robust, including visits and reunions. Whether they are my high school classmates or the Girl Scouts, we all know we share something very special, having grown up in Alaska during the 1950s. And many of us still search to understand how exactly this rare legacy has shaped us.

AUTHOR BIO

Ronda Stilley Kotelchuck.

Emerging from a childhood in the remote Alaskan community of Auke Bay, Ronda Stilley Kotelchuck received her undergraduate degree in psychology from Lewis and Clark College in Portland, Oregon. Seized by the ferment of the 1960s, she spent two years working in the civil rights movement, registering voters and building support for the movement on historically white campuses across the South. There she met and married her husband, David Kotelchuck. She obtained her master's degree at Cornell and, with her husband, settled in New York City and into a career in health care, with an abiding focus on social justice and bringing care to communities that would otherwise lack it.

She started out working for the activist Health Policy Advisory Center and became the editor of its muckraking Health/PAC Bulletin. She went on to work for the NYC Health and Hospitals Corporation, the City's massive municipal hospital system, rising to Vice President for Planning and Intergovernmental Affairs. Working with the Mayor's Office, she went on to found and run the highly successful Primary Care Development Corporation, a nonprofit organization promoting primary care in low income communities by providing affordable financing and technical assistance to community hospitals and community health centers across the nation. In 2015, she retired from that position after twenty-three years. Ms. Kotelchuck and her husband have lived for the last forty-eight years in New York City, where they raised their two daughters.

CPSIA information can be obtained
at www.ICGtesting.com
Printed in the USA
LVHW031756011019
632856LV00010B/848/P